FFH

Far From Home

FFH

Far From Home

Stories from the Road

HOWARD
PUBLISHING CO.

Our purpose at Howard Publishing is to:

- *Increase faith* in the hearts of growing Christians
- *Inspire holiness* in the lives of believers
- *Instill hope* in the hearts of struggling people everywhere

Because He's coming again!

01 02 03 04 05 06 07 08 09 10   10 9 8 7 6 5 4 3 2 1

Project editor, Philis Boultinghouse
Edited by Michele Buckingham
Interior design by Stephanie Denney
Cover design by LinDee Loveland
Photos on chapter opening pages by Kristin Barlowe. Used by permission.

Library of Congress Cataloging-in-Publication Data
FFH : Far From Home : stories from the road.
    p. cm.
  ISBN 1-58229-204-3
    1. FFH (Musical group) 2. Contemporary Christian musicians—Religious
life—United States. 3. Contemporary Christian musicians—United States.
  I. FFH (Musical Group)
ML421.F44 F44 2001
782.25'164'0922—dc21
[B]   2001039349

Scripture quotations not otherwise marked are taken from the Holy Bible, New International Version. Copyright © 1973, 1978, 1984 International Bible Society. Used by permission of Zondervan Bible Publishers. Other Scripture taken from the Holy Bible, New King James Version (NKJV), © 1982 by Thomas Nelson, Inc.

"Letters from the Road" are actual letters from fans of FFH. Names and identifying details in those letters and in the story "Angels in Disguise" have been changed to protect the privacy of those fans.

FFH's Mission Statement

To reach as many people
for Jesus Christ as we can,
as quickly as we can

Contents

About the Authors

Jeromy—Jeromy Shawn Deibler was born on August 19, 1974, in Lancaster, Pennsylvania. While at summer camp in 1991—between his junior and senior years of high school—Jeromy and his childhood friend Brian Smith, along with two other friends, put some songs together and formed a band to perform at camp. They never intended the group to go any farther than that, but requests began to come in, asking them to perform in other cities. At the end of the summer, Brian and Jeromy headed off to a great institute of learning. Brian stayed four years—and graduated. Jeromy stayed four weeks—and didn't. Returning home, Jeromy continued to write for FFH and took over managing the band full-time. Jeromy's most memorable event was the day he married the love of his life, and his most treasured possession is his wedding ring (ah…so romantic!).

Jennifer—Jennifer Lois Deibler was born in Hillsboro, Missouri, on June 14 (and she's not telling the year!). She was home-schooled after the seventh grade and plans to homeschool her own children someday. Jennifer loves horses and began riding when she was three years old and showing horses when she was nine. Her hidden claim to fame is that she once held the title Miss Missouri Rodeo Queen. When she first met Jeromy, she thought he was a "kid," but now she claims their wedding day as her most memorable life experience. Jennifer's favorite thing about being a part of FFH is the ministry—"seeing people come to know and grow closer to Jesus."

Michael—Michael Dean Boggs (nicknamed Boggsy) was born November 8, 1978, in Tulsa, Oklahoma. He loves all kinds of sports, fishing, and working out (what a hunk!). His music career began as a child when he drummed on pots and pans with pencils, while his dad sang and played the guitar. And now as a guitarist for FFH, his musical career has gone far beyond childhood dreams. Reading his Bible and praying throughout the day, along with being involved in an accountability team, are what keep his faith strong. Before becoming a member of FFH, Michael was pursuing a degree in theology. Being a part of FFH allows him to fulfill his desire to minister to others.

Brian—Brian Richard Smith was born on July 27, 1974, and grew up in Quarryville, Pennsylvania. He enjoys sports, CDs, computer stuff, Sega Dreamcast, and Batman memorabilia. His most memorable experience was his wedding day, when he married his high school sweetheart, Allyson Wright. The saddest day of his childhood was the day his dog Barnie had to be put to sleep. He cried all day, hugging him until his dad had to take Barnie away. Brian grew up in a musical family. When he was in elementary school, his choir director mom made him pick up the trumpet, which he still enjoys playing today. Her "gentle nudging" paid off, and when he went to college, he made her proud by getting a degree in music. Now a member of FFH, Brian says, "The only reason we do what we do is because God has called us to be on stage sharing the gospel with as many people as we can."

Foreword

by Richard Stevenson

The reason you're reading this book is that you know how gifted FFH is. What makes them so wonderful? It's not only that they have all sacrificed for the cause of Christ. It's not even that they are obedient to their calling and to God's will. The Father is delighted with FFH because they share His heart.

As pastor of The Great Commission Fellowship in Wilmore, Kentucky, I have the privilege of ministering to a congregation filled with the generation known as X. Contrary to the negative press on this generation, it is filled with young men and women who are authentically real, wholeheartedly devoted, and radically committed to Jesus Christ. I believe that this generation can bring in Christ's end-time harvest and see the earth flooded with God's glory.

Jeromy, Jennifer, Brian, and Michael are awesome examples of the best of this generation. I have had the honor of ministering with this group on numerous occasions, and I continue to receive spiritual blessing from their music and ministry. I know them well enough to tell you, beyond a shadow of a doubt, that the Father in heaven is delighted with these guys! The Bible says that our Father is not willing that any of His little ones perish (see 2 Peter 3:9). That's our Father's heart, and FFH lives to that beat. Through their music, message, and now through the words in this book, they share God's love, Christ's grace, and the presence and power of the Holy Spirit.

God is using FFH to see many who are "far from home" come to know the joy of God's family and the rest of His embrace. This book can take you there. It's the Father's heartbeat for you.

Richard M. Stevenson, President
Great Commission Churches International

Introduction

Writing this book has been an education and an adventure. But most of all, it's been an opportunity to share some of the awesome lessons we've learned while on the road touring as FFH.

In this book you'll see us as we are—flaws and all—and you'll get a glimpse into life on the road and how our faith is shaped and challenged daily. You'll read about special "fans" who have blessed us more than we have blessed them, and you'll see how life's seemingly mundane experiences are used by God to shape and mold us for His purpose.

FFH's mission is simple: *to reach as many people*

for Jesus Christ as we can, as quickly as we can. That is why we do what we do, and when we get off track—as we all tend to do sometimes—this is what brings us back to solid ground.

In addition to stories of our life on the road, this book also shares

- *life applications* showing how what we've learned can affect you as well
- *questions* that allow you to think about your own life story
- *scriptures* to feed your soul
- *letters* from individuals whom God has touched through our songs
- *fun facts* relaying miscellaneous information about the FFH gang

It is our prayer that this book build your faith and encourage you to adopt our mission as you live your life for our Lord: to reach as many people for Jesus Christ as we can, as quickly as we can.

God bless!

Listen,

I tell you a MYSTERY:
We **will not** all sleep,
but we will all be **changed**—
in a FLASH, in the **twinkling**
of an eye,
AT THE LAST TRUMPET.
For the **trumpet** will sound,
the **dead will be raised** imperishable, and
we will be changed.

—1 Corinthians 15:51–52

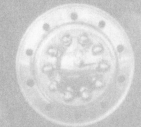

Tyson's Story

Michael Boggs

Looking around the bus, I picked out the faces of my fellow band members. Jeromy was sitting with his head back on a pillow; his wife, Jennifer, was nestled in close to him; and both were fading into a quiet sleep. Brian had on his headphones, listening to his Discman; and Allyson, his wife and our sound technician, was keeping herself busy reading a magazine. I leaned back comfortably, listening to the sounds of Shane Bernard coming through my headphones. I eventually decided to try to take a short nap, so I took off my headphones and laid my head against the edge of the window.

But sleep would not come. My mind refused to shut off. It was filled with thoughts of the reason for our trip and the night we had decided to come. After a concert just a few months ago, we had gathered inside the bus and, as usual, taken our places in the front lounge. We looked over the prayer requests from that night and began to pray for those who had gotten saved at the concert.

After we finished praying, Jeromy looked up and said that we had been asked to fly to California to sing for a man named Tyson, who had cancer and wasn't expected to live very long. He told us that Tyson enjoyed the song "One of These Days" and had requested that we sing it at church one Sunday morning. I had only been to California one time and was pretty excited just to go and see the place again. Everyone else was in favor of the trip as well, so we all agreed to go as soon as possible.

After the excitement of the idea of a California trip wore off, I began thinking about what I would say to Tyson when I saw him. I have never been around someone who was so close to eternity, and I wasn't quite sure how I would handle the awkwardness of that situation. What was I going to say to him? How could I pretend to be happy, knowing that this man had a wife, kids, friends, and family members who were going to miss him greatly when he was gone? Lying in my bunk that night inside that old, black Prevost bus, I began to get a little nervous about the trip to San Jose.

And now, with my head leaning against the bus window, I began to think about Tyson. What would I say? How would I react? Would I cry? I couldn't cry. I had to be strong and supportive in these situations, and besides, they just wanted us to sing a few songs; they weren't asking us to get personally involved with a man we didn't even know.

We stepped off the bus and headed straight to the church so that we could set up our equipment and do our sound check before the service started. As usual we made sure all the acoustic guitars worked, then following what has become somewhat of a tradition for us, Brian and I played a verse of "Power in His Blood," Jennifer ran through a tiny bit of "I'm Alright," Jeromy picked up his guitar and sang the scat to "Big Fish," and finally, we checked our tracks. It seemed to be a routine day, and we walked off the stage about thirty minutes before the service started.

Then suddenly the wooden doors to the sanctuary opened, and we saw a fragile man in a wheelchair slowly rolling toward us. It was Tyson. Immediately, my heart began to race and my palms began to sweat. I had decided to let my fellow band mates make the first move. They didn't let me down, and soon we engaged in a "get-acquainted" conversation with Tyson. I quickly found myself feeling comfortable with Tyson—almost as if I'd known him for a long while. Even though only a few minutes had passed, we knew that something special was about to happen between us and Tyson. As we talked with him, his voice began to lose power as he tired simply with talking. He reached out his weak hand to shake ours and softly asked, "You guys are going to sing 'One of These Days,' aren't you?"

FFH   Michael's favorite Bible verse is Matthew 16:24.

We all smiled and said, "Sure, if you still want us to."

"I would love for you to," he said, returning our smiles.

After meeting Tyson, I felt confident that God was about to do something big in that church that day, and I assumed it would be for Tyson. Maybe God would heal him. Maybe Tyson would instantaneously be free of pain, or maybe he would be healed over the course of several months. But as the day wore on I began to see that we were being more blessed than Tyson or anyone else in that church.

Soon the auditorium began to fill as people filed in for the morning worship. We began by singing an a capella song, then we meandered our way through the set list. It was a good day. We were all singing well and playing well, and we could see that Tyson was really enjoying himself. Every once in a while, he would smile or lift his hands up in the air expressing his love to the Father.

Finally the moment we had all been waiting for arrived. The next and last song was "One of These

Days," and we all looked at each other as if to say, "Let's give it our best shot"—and we did. The music started, and Jeromy began to sing the opening verse. My eyes were on Tyson to see what he would do. He weakly sang every word right along with Jeromy. For the first time in my life, I saw one of our songs take life. Here was a man who was obviously in a great deal of pain, singing the words to a song that to most of us is a distant possibility. For Tyson, it was current reality. "One of these days" was coming soon for him, and we all knew that. By the time the chorus came in, we were emotional wrecks; and to make matters even more intense, Tyson, whom they said hadn't stood in weeks, rose to his feet and lifted his hands in the air as if he could touch the floor of heaven. As tears filled the eyes of Jeromy, Brian, Jennifer, and me, we understood for the first time what "one of these days" really meant.

Before we left that day, we had a chance to talk again with Tyson and to give him somewhat of a private concert. At the time our record *Found a Place* wasn't completely finished, but we gave him a sneak preview of it and once again began to praise the Lord through song with Tyson.

Tyson never was healed of his cancer. In fact, just a short while after we sang to him, he passed away. While news of his death filled us all

For the first time in my life, I saw one of our songs take life.

with sadness, we knew that Tyson had not been afraid of eternity. He knew where he was going to spend it and whom he was going to spend it with. The simple smile from a man who was approaching the end of his life taught me a valuable lesson: When heaven is your home, you have no reason to fear, you have no reason to worry, and you have no reason to be alarmed at death because Jesus has already conquered it (see Revelation 1:18).

As I reflect on what I've written here, I can't help but think of Tyson sitting up in heaven some-where, maybe by the streets of gold or perhaps by the crystal sea, living out "one of these days."

One of these days
I'm gonna fly
over the MOUNTAIN
One of these days
I'm gonna ride
on the silver lining
One of these days
I'm gonna witness
all I've been missing
ONE OF THESE DAYS

God's Guestlist

Have you ever thought about the fact that one of these days, you, like Tyson, will meet your Creator and Judge face to face? Will your name be on His "guestlist" when you do? The Book of Romans tells us that all of us have sinned and fallen short of the glory of God and that the wages of sin is death. But the good news is that if we confess with our mouths that Jesus is Lord and believe in our hearts that God has raised Him from the dead, we will be saved (see Romans 10:9).

If you want to have a relationship with God, I would encourage you to pray this simple prayer of faith: "Father, I realize that I have failed You, and I know that my sin can keep me from spending eternity with You. I realize that Jesus is Your Son and that He died on a cross and rose again to forgive my sins so that I might have life after this life is through. So, God, I ask forgiveness for the things I have done wrong, and I ask You to come into my heart and be the Lord of my life once and for all. Amen."

If you prayed this prayer, I encourage you to tell a Christian friend or family member about it. I also suggest that you get a Bible and start reading in the Gospel of John; and finally, I challenge you to keep praying that God would grow you in your Christian walk.

No matter where you find yourself right now, no matter what you've done or how far you've strayed, God eagerly awaits your response to Him. It's up to you to accept His gift and allow Jesus to reign in your heart.

What's Your Story?

1. Are you ready for His return "one of these days"?
2. Did you see anything in the life of Tyson that you would like to imitate? What?
3. What scares you most about death? Why?
4. Are you on God's guestlist?
5. Have you ever prayed the prayer of faith?

Let us fix our eyes on Jesus, the **author** and PERFECTER of our **faith**, WHO FOR THE joy set before **him** ENDURED the CROSS, **scorning** its shame, and sat down at the RIGHT hand of the throne of God.

—Hebrews 12:2

Why Do I Do This?

Jennifer Deibler

It's four o'clock in the morning. I've just been rudely awakened by my alarm clock confirming what I knew when I fell asleep—I don't feel like getting up this early. I peel myself out of bed and begin to get ready for a long day of "meet and greet's," interviews, and radio spots, followed by a performance in front of key industry personnel. I begin to prepare for the day as I get dressed and put on the makeup that I will be wearing for the next twenty hours. I stupidly decide to go with jeans and sandals (with four-inch heels). Jeromy and I pack an overnight case and head to the airport. As we pull out of our driveway in the blackness of the night, I ask myself, *Why do I do this?*

Brian and Mike are waiting for us at the airport when we arrive. Jeromy and I go through our normal routine: He parks the car, I check the bags, and he meets me at the gate. We have done this way too many times. Our nonstop flight to Dallas departs at six o'clock. After a plain bagel and a can of orange juice, I catch a nap on the plane. We arrive in Dallas, where our radio promoter, Kyle, is waiting for us at the gate. He informs us that there will be no time to stop at the hotel to freshen up—we're running behind and need to get right to the convention center.

As we drive, Kyle gives us a brief rundown of the day's activities. First an early luncheon with a few VIP inspirational radio programmers—several of whom are not yet playing our single. If we make a good impression, they may give us a late add, ensuring that "Lord Move, or Move Me" will make it to number one. No pressure though. Lunch will be followed by an afternoon filled with radio and television interviews. We will try to have a quick sound check before dinner. Immediately after sound check we will attempt to meet the publisher of this book for a planning session. After a fancy meal with one of the country's largest Christian radio stations, we will have about fifteen minutes to change in a hotel bathroom and be backstage at the awards ceremony, where we will perform our two songs and present several lifetime achievement awards. We will be sure to get our pictures taken with John Tesh and Larry Burkett before heading to our hotel for a shower and a short night's sleep before our 6:00 A.M. flight back to Nashville.

As Kyle finishes up his rundown of the day, I stare blankly out the window of the rental van into the rainy Dallas sky. Again I ask myself, *Why do I do this?* We pull into the convention center parking lot, and I cover my head with a magazine as we run through the rain into the hotel lobby. I can feel my hair getting frizzy, and my feet are already starting to throb.

Lunch goes well, the Mexican buffet gives us a boost, and we're off to the interviews. First, a chat with George Carden, an interviewer and friend, about this past year on the road and the upcoming release. Next, the filming of a pilot for a PAX TV program followed by liners for a radio show whose title escapes me. We're behind schedule, so Kyle cuts the liners short and we run through the rain to the adjacent building for an interview with *Shine* magazine. Mike didn't eat any lunch because he can't stomach Mexican food, so Kyle and Michael Johnson (our Essential Records radio rep who joined us for the afternoon) try to find him a cookie along the way. Again I ask myself, *Why do I do this? And why did I wear these stupid shoes?*

We finally figure out that we are in the wrong building, so we run back to where we just were. Michael Johnson scores a brownie and a bag of chips along the way. Mike is happy for the time being. The *Shine* interview never happens, so we are back on schedule. On the way to a videotaping for a program in Canada, we are stopped by a few college students and asked for a video liner. Much to Kyle's disapproval, we do the liners and arrive at the makeshift taping studio in the middle of the convention floor in time to put on some makeup, which we now realize is still in the van. Allyson, Brian's wife and our sound technician, runs out to get it and returns just in time. By now my hair is totally frizzy and my makeup has completely worn off. Again I ask myself, *Why do I do this?*

As we take the platform and get microphones clipped onto our shirts, I look out over the growing

> Before she gets much farther, she starts to cry. She explains that she had been faithfully praying for her unsaved husband for years.

crowd of onlookers and I'm reminded of how nervous I get for TV stuff. By now I'm feeling pretty insecure about how I look. As I sit back in my chair and try to prepare for the upcoming questions, my body tells me how tired I really am. The interview is over as quickly as it starts, but before we could be whisked off of the platform, the interviewer asks if he could pray for our ministry. Knowing that his day is probably as crazy as ours, we appreciate the offer and pause for just a minute to ask the Lord's blessing. As I make my way down the platform, I am stopped by a woman who says she has something important to tell me. I know that time is short (Jeromy, Brian, and

Mike are already being pulled to the next inter-view), but something in her eyes tells me that this is more important than keeping the schedule, so I stay.

She begins by telling me that she had recently attended one of our shows. Before she gets much farther, she starts to cry. She explains that she had been faithfully praying for her unsaved husband for years. For some reason she was able to convince him to come to one of our concerts with her. That night, like in most of our concerts, Jeromy gave his testimony and invited people in the audience who hadn't given their lives to Jesus to pray the prayer of salvation with him. Her husband raised his hand, signifying his need for forgiveness, and repeated the sinner's prayer with Jeromy. She wipes the tears from her eyes and thanks me for our ministry. I give her a hug and thank her for sharing her story with me. As I walk away I feel as though the Lord whis-pers, "This is why you do this."

The rest of the day went as planned. Sound check was confusing, our meeting with Howard Publishing was cut short, and dinner with the radio station was rushed. The concert went without a

Jennifer was saved at age eight at a revival service.

hitch, and our first experience with a video teleprompter was a success. We left before the event was over and tried to get as much sleep as possible before our early morning flight back to Nashville. The guys from lunch never added our song, and no one knows what happened to the *Shine* interview. Strangely enough none of that seems important now. I know why I do this.

Why Do You Do It?

Throughout the New Testament, we see Jesus stopping in the middle of busy crowds to pay attention to a single onlooker who needed His touch. In the Gospel of Mark, it was the woman who touched the hem of his garment. In Matthew, it was the two blind men who called for healing. In Luke, it was the father for whom Jesus left the crowd to attend to his sick daughter. In Dallas, the Lord spoke to me in the middle of my distractions and reminded me of His greater purpose for my life.

The parable of the sower in Matthew 13 tells about how the distractions (weeds) of this life can choke our communication with God. God's words

EVE

Every now and then
I get a little
wrapped up in myself
And I can't see You
reaching
Every now and then
I get a little
overwhelmed by the world
And I can't **hear** You calling
But You have always told me
You will always be there
You are only
one PRAYER away

every now

You are
one only prayer AWAY

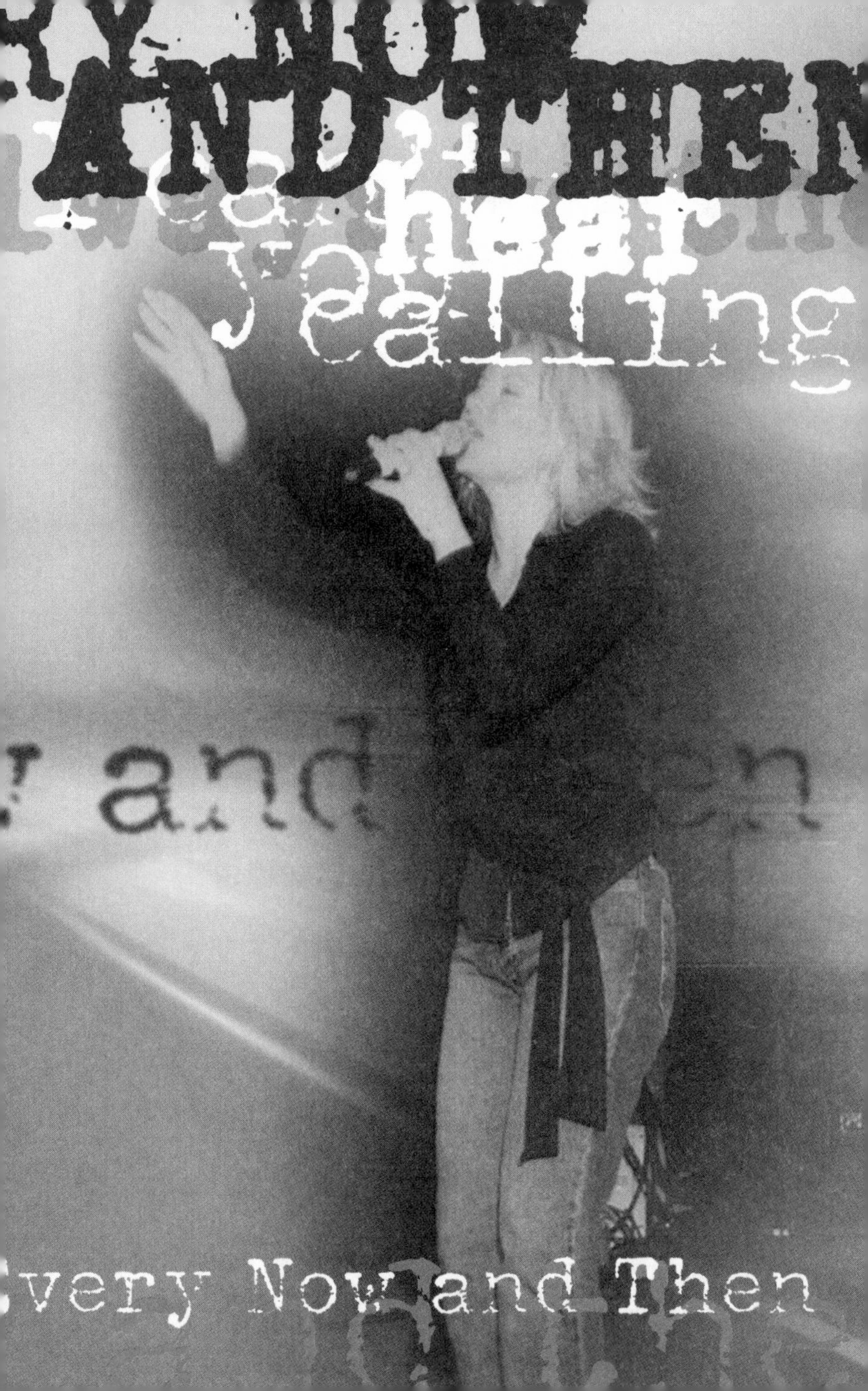

AND THEN
hear
calling
and
very Now and Then

to us are like seeds, and when they fall among our ever-present busy schedules, they are harder to recognize and distinguish. As believers, we have a responsibility to rid ourselves of things that keep us from hearing God's voice. The writer of Hebrews exhorts us to cast off the things of this life that so easily entangle us so that we might run this "race of faith" and fix our eyes on Jesus. I encourage you to pray today that the Lord might show you the things in your life that are keeping you from hearing his voice. For me it is my schedule and TV. For you it might be career, household distractions, or just plain busyness. Whatever the case may be, God is longing to have your attention—even amidst the craziness of this world.

What's Your Story?

1. When was the last time you stopped in the middle of a busy day to bless the life of another? How did it make you feel? How do you suppose it made God feel?

2. What, in your life, keeps you from hearing

God's voice? What can you do to remove that distraction?

3. Do you know anyone who always seems to make time for other people? What can you do to imitate that person?

Letters from the Road

Dear FFH,

You guys will always have a special place in my heart as well as my ear. For the first two years of my marriage, I tried to get my wife to church. We happened to go by Berean bookstore one time, and to my surprise, she was very interested in looking around. Then the best thing happened! We heard this band called FFH!! She fell in love with your music. Since then she has been saved and our whole marriage, family, and everything has just been better and better. The Lord works through you guys, and I just wanted to say thank you from the bottom of my and my children's hearts. The next big step for us is to see you guys in concert. We would love to praise God with you so we can all "throw our hands up in the air" and praise God. Your music moves people closer to Jesus!

Thank you and God bless you guys, Joseph

Pray also for ME, that whenever I **OPEN MY MOUTH**, words may be given me so that I will fearlessly make **known** the mystery of the GOSPEL, for which I am an AMBASSADOR in chains. **PRAY THAT I MAY DECLARE** it fearlessly, as I **should**.

—Ephesians 6:19–20

Stepping on God's Toes

Jeromy Deibler

3

Since our beginning in 1991, FFH has played in all sorts of venues for all sorts of people. Our first-ever performance was at a family camp in Lancaster, Pennsylvania, and much of those first few years were spent touring around southeastern Pennsylvania, performing in small churches and campgrounds. During those years, numbers were not important. If someone was listening, we would sing.

I remember driving eight hours from Lancaster across Highway 81 to Knox, Pennsylvania, carrying a full sound rig, only to set up and play for three people. We once drove our van to Kentucky for a weekend of shows to play for sixteen people on Friday and eleven on Saturday. The promoter didn't consider that homecoming weekend in a town of fifteen hundred people might not be the most appropriate time for a concert! For seven years, we traveled up and down the East Coast wearing out Route 95 playing concerts to whoever would attend.

We realize now that God was using those experiences to prepare us for what was to come. He taught us that whether we were in front of fifty people or five thousand, He expected us to give it all we had. He also taught us that no matter what the situation, it is always appropriate to present the gospel.

We thank the Lord every time we pray together for bringing our ministry to where it is today. We love playing and singing and would still do it for whoever is listening, but it sure is nice playing to packed houses and sold-out auditoriums. However, the Lord is still teaching us about who we are and that He expects us to be consistent.

During the past year or two, the Lord has opened several doors for us to perform at professional sporting events. Typically, the audience pays to see whatever game is being played. Following the game, they enjoy a miniconcert. The events are a lot of fun to play because the games are exciting and the crowds are huge. It was at one of these postgame concerts in Charlotte where our consistency was tested.

We weren't even supposed to do any concerts in early March. We, along with our manager, had informed our booking agent that we needed all of January and February and much of March to record our new album. Then the offer for the Charlotte game came through. We decided to play the date, allowing ourselves a break from the studio. It was a way for us to get away from Nashville and clear our heads.

We left town at midnight the night before the show. When I woke up, we were parked in front of the arena. There's something special about looking out the window of the bus first thing in the morning and seeing a towering arena, knowing that we are about to fill it with sound. The day went as planned: a catered lunch followed by a trip to the hotel, a relaxing jog and a shower, then back to the arena for sound check. Just before sound check, I had a chance to talk to the promoter about how he wanted the evening to go. He was excited about the expected crowd and told me some specifics.

Normally in these miniconcert events, there is not time for an invitation or a time of sharing. Since the concert typically doesn't start until 10:30 or 11:00 P.M., they ask us to pack as many "hits" into the allotted time as possible. However, I thought it wouldn't hurt to ask him if we could try to squeeze in an invitation. Surprisingly, he said yes and said that as long as we are out by midnight, we would be fine. The four of us, along with our crew, ended up walking to a nearby restaurant for dinner. As we were eating I asked everyone if they thought we should try to fit the invitation into the set. Everyone agreed that we shouldn't pass up the opportunity to present the gospel to this many non-Christians, so I began thinking about how we could work it into the abbreviated concert.

The game ended on time, Charlotte won, and everyone was happy. Moreover, almost the entire crowd seemed to stay for the show. After about thirty minutes of setup and another forty-five for

Jeromy can wink with his left nostril.

an opening act, we were set to take the stage. We could feel the energy from the crowd as we were introduced and walked up to the platform that was resting on the ice. The set went great, and before I knew it we were starting our second-to-last song, "Daniel." As the song ended, I glanced at my watch and realized that we were running out of time.

Almost as if I had gone brain-dead, I nodded to Allyson, our monitor tech, and signaled to her we would be starting "One of These Days"—our closer. Jennifer, Brian, and Mike all looked at me like I was crazy. The music began playing in my in-ear monitors and I started to sing, not knowing that the audience wasn't hearing anything. I glanced off the stage at Allyson and recognized that she was trying to tell me something. Instinctively, I popped out one of my in-ears and realized that I was singing but no music was coming out. Out of courtesy, some of the audience had begun to sing along with this a cappella version of "One of These Days."

My heart began to pound and my palms began to

Now I want to
be used by YOU,
so make me able
And I want to be
CLOSE TO YOU,
so keep me humble
Cause I know what
You need from me
Is a lot less of me
So go ahead and
take the best of me
And change the rest of me

so keep me
humble

sweat, not because I didn't know what to do, but because I realized that I had stepped on God's toes and had gotten in His way. I immediately quieted the crowd, and not knowing exactly what to say, I apologized to them for not following God's call. I bore my heart on my sleeve and explained to all ten thousand listeners that God had told me to give an invitation, but that I got lazy and didn't do it. Uncharacteristically, I was at a loss for words.

After a pregnant pause, Mike instinctively picked up his guitar, found a key, and began to try to fill the dead air. I joined in on a chorus of "I Exalt Thee." After about ten minutes of some of the sweetest worship that we have ever been a part of, I presented the gospel and gave folks a chance to give their hearts to Jesus. More than thirty people raised their hands and prayed the prayer of salvation. After a few short words of encouragement, we sang "One of These Days," took a bow, and got off the stage—at 12:30 A.M. As soon as I could, I found the promoter and apologized for the mess. Nobody got fined or went to jail, and I walked out of the arena having learned an important lesson.

Being on God's Page

We know that God speaks. Deuteronomy 8:3 says that "man does not live on bread alone but on every word that comes from the mouth of the LORD." We

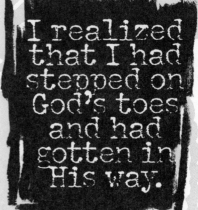

I realized that I had stepped on God's toes and had gotten in His way.

know that the Holy Spirit is at work guiding us in God's will. We read in the Gospel of John that the Spirit of Truth has come and that He will guide us into all truth. However, when we let our own personal agenda get in the way of God's plan, we quench the Spirit (see 1 Thessalonians 5:19). To "quench" means to put a stop to or cool suddenly.

When we get in God's way and stop the Spirit's work, we can adversely affect people's eternity. That's why, as believers, our obedience to God's will and resistance to our own is so important. God didn't care that we went past midnight. He didn't care that we were embarrassed when the system failed and we looked like amateurs. He was not anxiously tapping His watch hoping that I would allow time for the invitation. He had planned on people getting saved. He knew that March 9, 2001, was going to be the night that more than thirty folks from North Carolina received eternal life. I had agreed to that plan. God assumed that I was on His page.

When my laziness got in the way, God's plan didn't change. Fortunately I had the spiritual presence of mind to recognize what was going on and get back in line with God's flow. If not, who knows, maybe God would have taken me out of the situation and Brian would have given the invitation. There's a scary thought!

There are many days when I feel out of sync with God and His direction. I feel disconnected. In these times of indecision, my first reaction is to just do something and hope that God steers me down His path. As believers, we have to fight this temptation. God has a specific design for our lives. If we don't get ahead of Him and if we try not to step on His toes, we will find life a much more enjoyable journey. We won't find ourselves onstage in front of thousands of people wondering what to say next.

What's Your Story?

1. Have you ever felt "out of sync" with God? What caused you to fall behind? How did you get back in line with His will? If you're still out of sync, what can you do to obey His will for your life?

2. Are you ever embarrassed to speak up for God? What kind of situations cause this embarrassment in you?

3. What can you do differently the next time you are given an opportunity to speak a word for God?

Letters from the Road

Hi guys!

I attended your concert last night and it was awesome! I took two of my three kids and a friend, and I just wanted to let you know that our friend came to know Jesus last night through your ministry. What you are doing is truly a gift from God. Thank you for who you are and what you are doing!

God bless you all!

Mary

The LORD is my STRENGTH and my song; HE has become my salvation. He is my GOD, and I will PRAISE him, my FATHER'S God, and I will exalt Him.

—Exodus 15:2

Practicing for Heaven

Brian Smith

We arrived at the mall a few hours before the concert was to begin and found people already waiting for the event. We were surprised to see so many people so soon but also excited to think that people might actually show up for this show after all. The concert was part of the Dallas radio station's Brown Bag Luncheon series. Basically, it was a free concert for people to enjoy during their lunch break—they could eat, relax, and listen to music. I thought it seemed like a great idea, but we had never performed in a mall before, so we had no idea what to expect.

That morning we woke up really early. In fact, it was still dark outside. For some reason, radio interviews are always at the crack of dawn. Shortly after the interview, they whisked us off to the mall so we could get ready for the concert.

The mall security took us to a behind-the-scenes room so we could eat lunch and get ready. It felt kind of weird to have security take us everywhere. We were not accustomed to big crowds and people wanting our autographs. This was our first time in Dallas, and so far it was going great. After a quick sound check, we again went backstage to wait for the concert. By now, there were quite a few people in the mall, but we didn't know if they were there to see us or to shop. It seemed like forever until showtime, and we had no idea what waited for us downstairs.

Finally, it was time to go onstage, and security surrounded us for the trek to the platform. I remember thinking to myself, *Come on, what is this for? To protect us from the ten people that are here today to see us?* As we rounded the corner near the stage, our jaws almost dropped. There in front of us were tons of people. As we made our way down the

Brian's fondest childhood memory is the day his family adopted his sister.

escalator, we felt as if we were in a dream—people were everywhere. The mall area consisted of two floors. The stage was located in the middle of the first floor, which was round with hallways branching off either side. When we looked up to see the second floor, we saw a circular area that was railed all the way around. Our host introduced us, and we walked up on the platform. From the stage, we saw a sea of people. People were all around us, so we had to continually change our direction in order to interact with the crowd. As I looked around, I couldn't find an empty spot in the whole place. People were crammed in as far as I could see on the bottom level, and on the top, people were hanging over the railing just trying to get a glimpse of the stage. It was amazing. Nothing we had ever done was quite like this.

About halfway through our set, we decided to lead the crowd in some praise-and-worship music. We were a little nervous about doing this and really didn't know what kind of reaction we'd get. But we love singing praise-and-worship songs with our audiences and felt that today's concert should be no different. Our praise-and-worship sets are very simple. We sing songs that everyone can sing along with us. We started out with some of the most familiar choruses such as "I Exalt Thee," "Step by Step," and so on.

Looking around at the audience, I saw that almost everyone was singing and worshiping God. It seemed huge. I stepped back from my microphone and tried to take it all in. I looked over the crowd and saw eyes closed and hands raised. It was incredible. I glanced over at Jeromy, and we exchanged expressions of disbelief. Here we were crammed in a public mall, with shops everywhere, leading praise and worship for three thousand people on their lunch break. It felt like a preview of heaven. The sound was amazing.

We all stepped back from our microphones and let the crowd take over. The sound echoed off the mall walls and filled the atrium. There was no doubt that the sound of people praising God was sweeping through the entire mall. At that moment, I knew that God's presence was there. I wished that time would stand still.

I will always remember that moment. It has forever changed my point of view about praise and worship. It was practice for heaven. The sound of God's people praising Him in such a public place was awesome.

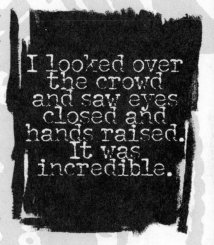

I looked over the crowd and saw eyes closed and hands raised. It was incredible.

Believe it or not, after Jeromy's quick testimony, three people came back to our table wanting to make decisions. It was awesome to see God use the praise-and-worship time to soften the hearts of those people and plant some seeds in their hearts. It was also incredible to see the eyes of the audience quickly taken off of us and focused on the Creator—where they should be.

We realized that day that there is nothing special about us being up there, unless we lift up the name of our Creator and praise Him. Ever since that experience, we lead God's people in praise and worship at all of our concerts.

because of

Far From Home

mountain peaks
oceans wide

BECAUSE OF

who you are

The mountain peaks,
the oceans wide
They speak Your name,
they testify
To all that is
and all that was
and all that is to come
You're the
GREAT I AM,
You're the
Holy One
You're the
One and only Son of God

Because of Who You Are

God Inhabits Praise

Why is it that we are surprised to find that God actually shows up when we call upon His name? The Bible tells us in Psalm 22:3 that God inhabits praise. That means that He lives in praise. When we began to praise God at the Arlington Parks Mall, it should have been no surprise that His presence descended upon that place. Other versions of Psalm 22:3 say that God is enthroned upon the praises of Israel. The praises of His people actually become His throne.

Do you want God to be where you are? Then praise Him. Lift your voice to Him. Sing a song; say a prayer. Tell Him how wonderful and powerful and mighty He is. Not because He needs to hear it from you, but because you need to be in His presence.

There is a certain power in praising God—an undeniable strength. Do you remember the Old Testament character Nehemiah, who led the Israelites in rebuilding the wall of Jerusalem after years of Babylonian captivity? After the completion of the wall, Nehemiah called an assembly of all the people. There he read the book of the Law, which had not been read in years. Upon hearing it, the people wept. But Nehemiah told them, "Do not grieve, for the joy of the LORD is your strength" (Nehemiah 8:10). Do you sometimes feel weak and unable to handle the stresses of your life? Overwhelmed by past failures, distressed by current circumstances? This verse tells us that we can find strength in joy!

What's Your Story?

1. Why is praise-and-worship music important? What is its purpose?

2. Have you ever felt God's presence in a situation where you really hadn't expected Him to show up?

3. How can we praise God other than through singing?

For **YOU** created MY inmost being;
you knit me TOGETHER
in my **mother's womb**.
I **praise** you because I am fearfully
and **wonderfully made**;
your WORKS are **wonderful**,
I know that full well....
ALL the days **ordained** for me
were written in **your book**
before ONE of them **came to be.**

—Psalm 139:13–14, 16

Finding My Place

Michael Boggs

5

I was attending a small Bible college when the school's director of recruitment asked me to travel to a recruiting conference in the tiny town of Roach, Missouri. I'd made this same trip the year before and told the director I'd be happy to tag along and help in any way that I could. I was nineteen years old, and I really enjoyed visiting different places and telling other young people about our school. Little did I know that I was about to embark on a journey that would change my life.

I packed a small duffel bag, my guitar, and my Bible, and a group of us set out on the road trip. We

47

must have sung at least thirty songs on the way to Roach. We were especially excited because we'd learned that a Christian band named FFH would be at the conference. We had heard the group at the same event the previous year, so we fully expected to have a great time.

Finally we pulled into the driveway and unloaded all of our stuff. We took our banners and pamphlets and other recruiting materials and walked into the auditorium to set up our display. To my surprise, FFH was already in the auditorium, setting up the sound equipment for their concert that night. I was in a small band back home, so I was very interested to see how the professionals worked. I stood and watched, totally captivated. My college group quickly realized that I was going to be of no help to them, and they encouraged me to ask if FFH needed any assistance.

That's when I noticed that one of the band members, Steve, was having some technical problems with his guitar. When I saw him begin to take his guitar apart, I casually walked up and asked him if he wanted to borrow my guitar for the concert that night.

"I'd like to see the guitar," he said, "and if you don't mind, I might take you up on that offer."

I quickly ran to get my guitar. When I handed it to Steve, I could see that he liked it. *This is the coolest thing in the world,* I thought. *A guy from FFH is going to play my guitar in an actual concert!*

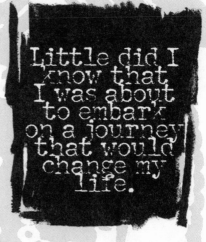

Little did I know that I was about to embark on a journey that would change my life.

But then things suddenly got cooler. "Maybe after the concert," Steve said, "we can play a couple of songs together." I could hardly contain my excitement. *Can life get any better than this? I don't think so!*

The concert that night was great, but all I could think about was getting to play some music with Steve afterward. Would he remember his invitation? After the concert ended and he finished signing autographs, I began making my way toward the stage.

Steve was fiddling around with my guitar. He looked up and smiled. "Want to play a little?" he said.

"Yes!" I responded, with obvious enthusiasm.

Steve and I played four or five songs together. I was so into the music that I didn't notice that the other band members were listening. Finally, when it was quite late, Steve said he needed to go and get some rest so he'd be ready for another concert the next day.

What a perfect night, I thought. *It can't get any better than this.* But it did. As Steve turned and walked away, another band member, Jeromy, approached me. He asked me about my life and what I thought God was calling me to do. We talked for a while, and then Jeromy asked me a startling question: Would I pray about how God might use me in the ministry of FFH?

"Why?" I asked, somewhat confused.

"I'm sorry to leave you hanging, but I can't say any more than that," he apologized. "For now, just pray about it."

The next day I returned to college and began praying about what Jeromy had said. I asked a few friends what they thought he'd meant, but no one had an answer. The idea crossed my mind that Jeromy might want to ask me to join the band, but I quickly dismissed the thought as either arrogant or delusional. After about two weeks, the curiosity was killing me. I called Jeromy and asked, "What's going on?"

"Have you been praying?"

"Yes," I said, "but I haven't really known how to pray about the situation."

"Just keep praying the way you have been," he said, "and I'll call you soon."

True to his word, Jeromy called before too long. He explained that Steve had felt called to leave the band and help start a church in his hometown in Pennsylvania. Then he asked if I would be interested in flying to Nashville, meeting with the group, and practicing with them for a few days.

Thrilled, I quickly agreed and tried to book the next flight out of Tulsa. I muddled through a series of late planes and cancelled flights before finally arriving in Nashville and stepping into a car with

Jeromy and Brian. My excitement turned to nervousness when Jeromy stated that he wanted to go ahead and practice a little that night. My ears were stopped up from the long plane ride, and I was sure that my performance was going to be subpar.

I ended up playing for the band, their manager, their producer, their record company, and their radio guy before I left that weekend. I had never been so nervous so many times in such a short period! But I must have done OK. Before I left to go back to Oklahoma, FFH asked me to become a member of their group.

I knew I wanted to join FFH. But was that what God wanted me to do? And what about college? I really enjoyed being a student, but I would have to quit school for a while to go on the road with the group. I spent many nights with family and friends, praying about the decision. FFH said they didn't expect an answer right away; in fact, they invited me to simply go on the road with them for a few days to see what it was like.

I accepted their invitation, and the rest is his-

Michael names his guitars—Big Mac, Little Mac, and Daddy Mac.

tory. The next time I went home to Tulsa, I packed my things and told my parents I was moving to Nashville. I didn't have a place to stay there, so Jeromy told me I could live with him and Jennifer until I could find and settle into a place of my own.

One night I sat in Jeromy's office playing my guitar while he and Jennifer watched television in the next room. A song began coming to me that seemed to be a confirmation from God that I was supposed to join the band. I called to Jeromy and asked him to come and listen to what I had written so far. He did, and an hour later we had completed the song "Found a Place."

There are still times when I ask myself, *What am I doing here? Why did God choose to use me this way?* All I know is that when God leads, we'd better follow. It was really hard for me to move ten hours away from family and friends and be completely on my own for the first time in my life. But I knew I had found my place with FFH—the place that God had been preparing for me since the day I was born.

I've found a place
where I can rest
I've found a place
of **sweet relief**
I've found a place
where I can hear
You whisper to me
I see the **writing**
on the wall
I realize that after
all is said and done—
That You are holding
E T E R N I T Y

Where I can
rest

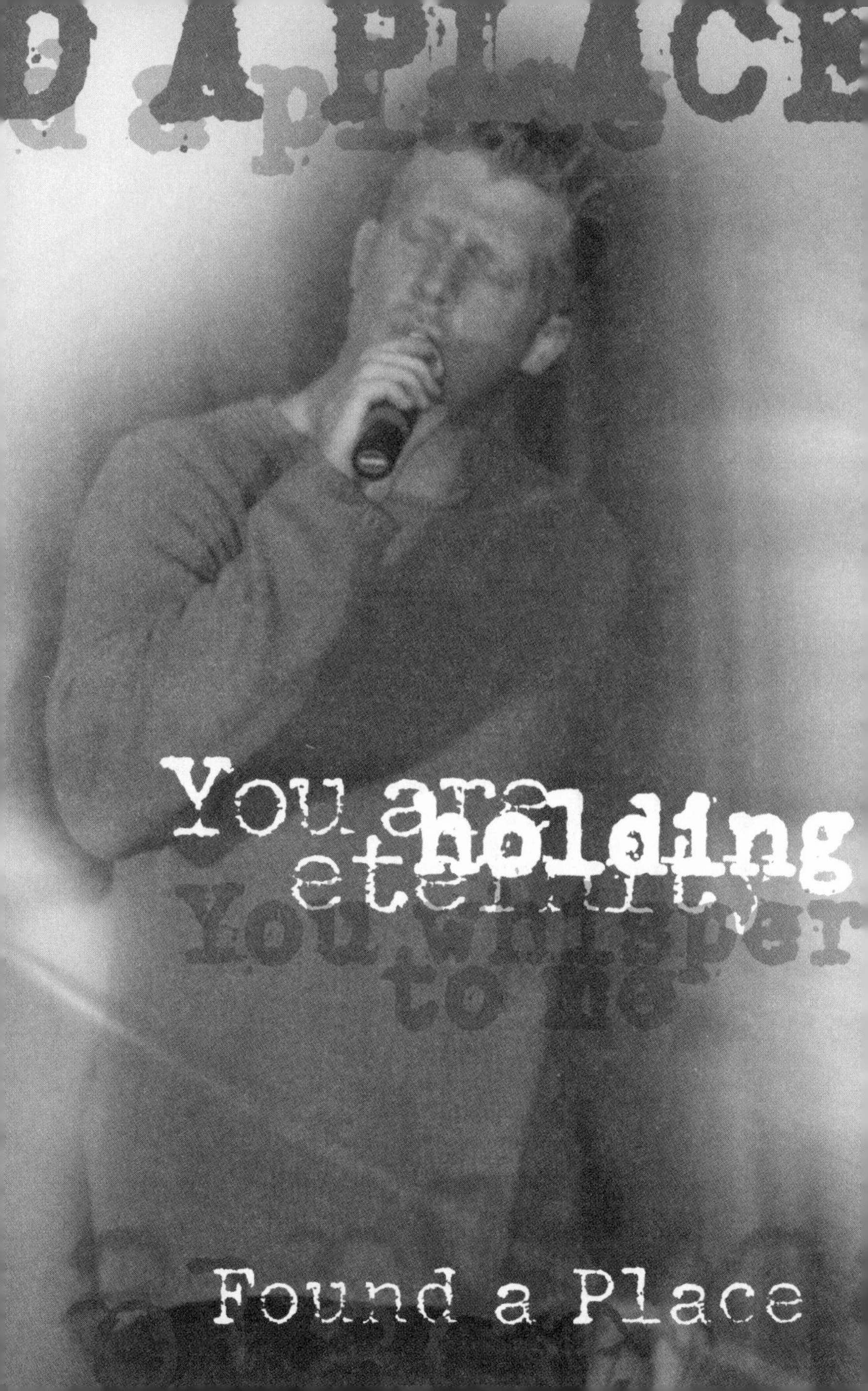
You are
holding
Found a Place

Where's Your Place?

Just as God had been preparing me all along to become part of FFH, He has been preparing you for something special since the day you were born. Who knows? Maybe you'll be a company president, a social worker, a teacher, an artist, a mom, or a dad. The point is that whatever God has planned for you, at this very moment He is molding you for that place.

What does God want you to do in your life? Have you asked Him? If you haven't, you need to. But remember that God doesn't always tell us exactly where He wants us to go. Sometimes He just tells us to hold His hand and go with Him, one step at a time. He has a specific destination in mind; we just need to trust Him to lead us there. God wants to direct our lives, and if we'll let Him, the possibilities of what we can do for Christ are endless!

The Scripture says, "The steps of a good man are ordered by the LORD, and He delights in his way" (Psalm 37:23 NKJV). Do you believe that? God has a chosen path for you, and He wants the two of you to walk down that road together. If you make it the primary ambition of your life to follow the Lord, you can trust Him to make sure you will find your place.

What's Your Story?

1. Do you know your "place" in life? Have you asked God to show it to you?

2. What doors has God opened for you that have guided you to where you are right now? What doors has He closed?

3. What is your primary ambition in life?

Letters from the Road

Hey guys and gal!

I just wanted to write and tell you all how much your music has meant to me over the years. Your first CD was one of the first Christian CDs I ever owned, and it has really changed my life. My friend Alice and I used to listen to "Big Fish" and "One of These Days" every morning on the way to school.

Since seeing you in concert, I have given my life to the Lord. Thank you for obeying the call of the Lord. I will pray for you all.

Gary

I run in the
PATH of YOUR COMMANDS,
for YOU HAVE
set my heart
free.

—Psalm 119:32

Heeding God's Voice

Jeromy Deibler

6

One mid-November day on a four-hour drive from St. Louis to a conference center in Windermere, Missouri, Steve approached the rest of us and asked if he could share some news. Immediately we assumed that he and his wife, Andrea, were going to inform us that they were expecting a child. That would have been easier to stomach than what we were about to hear.

Steve started by telling how much he loved FFH and how much the other six of us who made the road trips together meant to him. He also warned us that he was as surprised at what God was telling him as we would be. Steve then broke the news that he and Andrea would be leaving FFH. He didn't know when, why, or how, but he had been given a clear word from God that he was being called out of FFH to be involved in God's work somewhere else. Andrea nodded in agreement as they continued to tell us what they felt God was telling them to do. "I don't understand the whole thing," Steve said. "All I know is that God is calling me out of this."

After a few more minutes of explanation, a strange calm fell over the motor home. No one said much as we pulled into the conference center where we would be spending the next forty-eight hours. The youth conference would start in a few hours, and we needed to set up, so we put the conversation on hold until we could come together again as a group. Jennifer's dad, our road pastor, encouraged us not to worry and to know that God had a plan and was capable of seeing it through.

Steve dropped this news in the fall of 1998. At that time, we were touring nonstop all over the country, riding a wave of overnight success follow-ing our first national album release, *I Want to Be like*

You. Steve's wife, Andrea, worked with us selling our merchandise.

It was a crazy time for us. Brian's wife, Allyson, was our sound tech and was becoming quite good. Jennifer's mom drove the motor home, and her dad

> He didn't know when, why, or how, but he had been given a clear word from God that he was being called.

was the crew. Crowds were becoming huge, and we were starting to feel the effects of signing a record contract. We would pull into a town and hear ourselves on the radio. Audiences would come to shows with most of the songs memorized. Everyone in the band and crew was overextended, but we were handling the pressure. It was a season I will never forget.

Later that day I had the chance to talk with Steve a little more. As the leader of FFH, I knew it would be my responsibility to guide us through the details of this possible transition. I explained to Steve that the timing and uncertainty of the whole thing made me nervous. I needed him to confirm for me point-blank that his leaving was a "when" and not just an "if." He told me he was definitely leaving; it was just a matter of when. He also assured me that his love for FFH was stronger than ever and that he would never do anything to compromise the effectiveness of our ministry. He committed to staying until we found the right replacement. Little did we know that his replacement was in the next room.

The first night of the conference was a success. It was our second year in a row at Windermere, so the crowd warmed up to us right away. We performed a forty-five–minute set followed by a sweet time of worship. After the speaker closed his invitation, the seven hundred kids in attendance filed out of the building and headed for their cabins. The four of us and our crew hung around the auditorium for a while to catch up with some of the folks we had met the year before.

As I was talking with the promoter, who is also a good friend of mine, my attention was diverted to a group of people playing and singing by the front of the stage. My conversation with the promoter ended, and out of curiosity I made my way back to the front of the auditorium to see what was going on.

Steve was playing guitar with a few of the students

from the sponsoring Bible college, and some folks were standing around them in a circle. As I turned the corner, I noticed that facing Steve was a young red-haired fellow with a goatee. They were swapping Michael's guitar back and forth, teaching each other their favorite licks. I asked a friend of mine who the fellow was. He told me that he was a student at the college. His name was Mike Boggs—"Boggsy" to all of his friends. I thought very little about the encounter that night. The next day, however, was a different story.

Jennifer and I woke up just in time to play our 9:00 A.M. worship set. After the speaker had finished, the college band went onstage to play some games. Michael played guitar for several of the activities, and I began to notice that he was rather good.

Then it happened. I was on my way to the lower level of the auditorium to use the rest room when almost audibly God spoke to me and said, "Ask Mike Boggs to be in FFH." I know it sounds crazy, but it had to be God because I didn't even know Mike. We had never even talked! As soon as I could put the pieces of the moment together, I told Brian. He trustingly said, "OK, say something to him. Let's see what happens."

So that night, just before we pulled out of the conference center to head back to Nashville, I found Mike and pulled him aside. I was still unsure about what God was doing, so I said, "Mike, I want you to pray about how God might use you in FFH." That was all I felt comfortable saying at the time. His eyes got huge, and he looked at me in stunned confusion and said, "OK, but I don't get it." We exchanged numbers, and I told him I would call him as soon as I could. Again, I urged him to pray about it.

We left the conference center and headed home. Jennifer and I stopped off in St. Louis for Thanksgiving with her family, and the rest of the group headed back to Nashville in the motor home. Steve still hadn't told many people about his new direction, so out of courtesy I kept it to myself. Mike called me a few days later; the curiosity was killing him. I told him I couldn't give him any more information and again told him to keep praying about it.

In December, Steve told me that it was OK to talk about his plans. I immediately called Mike and told him the details of how we wanted him to consider replacing Steve in FFH. When Mike came to

FFH's *Found a Place* CD has been to space, thanks to an eleven-year-old girl.

Nashville and played with us, Jennifer, Brian, and I felt God's confirmation that Mike was a good replacement. Mike had already been praying about it, so he was ready to agree immediately. Mike's parents were surprisingly in agreement as well. That next month, Mike quit college and moved into our guest room. For a month we lived together, getting to know each other and working on FFH songs as well as some new ones of our own. Two weeks later Mike was onstage, and the rest is history.

A few months later, Steve and Andrea moved to Huntingdon, Pennsylvania, to be part of a church plant. Things are going well, and they are seeing God move in miraculous ways. We talk once every couple of months and fill each other in on what is happening in our lives. Inevitably we end up reminiscing about those special years and how God was preparing us for what was to come.

He Knows What's on the Other Side

At no other time in my life has God's direction been as unmistakably clear as it was during those

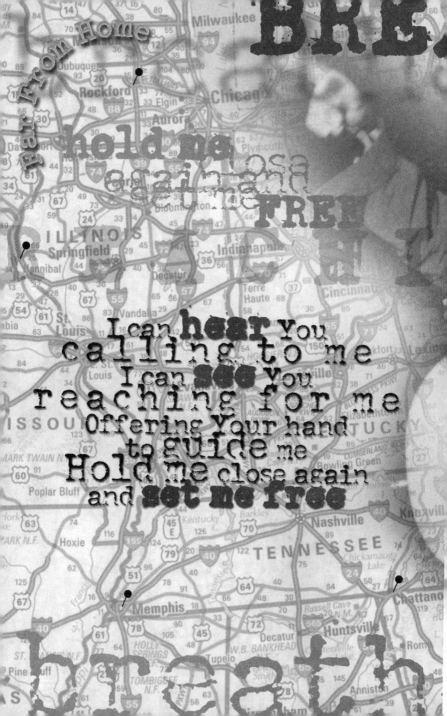

I can **hear** You
calling to me
I can **see** You
reaching for me
Offering Your hand
to **guide** me
Hold me close again
and **set me free**

few months when Steve left and we replaced him with Mike. God taught me that not only is He walking with me through whatever I am currently going through, He is also already on the other side, preparing for me a new path. Romans 8:28 makes perfect sense to me now: "And we know that in all things God works for the good of those who love him, who have been called according to his purpose." God is always at work. He can make good out of any situation we face—if we are obedient to Him. And those of us who love Him and are following His call will experience His goodness in ways that we can never imagine.

My father-in-law and I have talked about this time and time again. I sometimes struggle with how big God is and how He allows these seemingly bad things to happen to us. Dad explained to me that we see life go by much like a parade. We can't see the floats coming until they round the corner. We see them most clearly when they are directly in front of us. Then, as they fade into the horizon, they again go out of focus. We are only able to concentrate on the things that are closest to us. God, however, sees the parade from above, much like He's looking at it from a helicopter. He's not surprised at what comes our way. He's able to allow things to happen because He knows what is on the other side.

What's Your Story?

1. When was the last time God surprised you with a turn of events you weren't expecting? Were you able to respond in faith and wait on Him or did you panic? What would you do differently next time?

2. Do you spend any really "quiet" time with God so that you can *listen* to His words? What have you heard Him say in such times? How can you set aside time just for you and Him to converse?

3. What does it mean that God is not only walking with you through whatever you are currently experiencing, but that He is also already on the other side, preparing a new path for you? What evidence of this truth have you seen in your life?

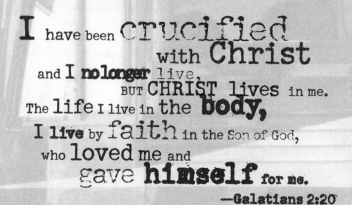

I have been crucified with Christ and I no longer live, BUT CHRIST lives in me. The life I live in the body, I live by faith in the Son of God, who loved me and gave himself for me.

—Galatians 2:20

The Nightmare Concert

Brian Smith

7

It was a typical morning on the road for FFH. After driving all night (well, our bus driver was driving; we were sleeping!), we arrived at our next venue in Baker, Louisiana. We awoke to a windy, overcast day. The crew got up before everyone else, then the rest of us rolled out of bed one by one.

I was the last one up that morning—just in time for lunch. I have to admit it's tough for me to crawl out of my warm bunk when I'm on the road. It's like being in bed at home and getting up to use the bathroom on a cold, dreary, winter morning. As soon as I step barefoot onto the frigid floor, I want to jump right back into the pile of warm blankets! Fortunately, my wife, Allyson, is a member of the FFH crew. When we're on the road she is always up way before me, and she loves me enough to make sure I don't sleep through lunchtime.

The rest of the day seemed to fly by. Setup went smoothly, the meals were great, and we had a chance to rest at the hotel. Later, as Jeromy, Jennifer, Michael, and I took our places on the concert stage and prepared for the sound check, we held our breath, hoping everything would sound OK. It had been more than a month since we'd done a show. We were glad to be out on the road again, but we definitely didn't have our touring groove down yet. Personally, I was praying that I would remember all the words to the songs! It's strange how things that usually come so naturally seem tough when you've been away from them for a while.

Jeromy checked, Mike checked, I checked, and Jennifer finished it out. The process went quickly, and everything sounded great in the ear monitors. I had lots of drums, lots of bass, and my vocal was cutting through. We gave Allyson the thumbs-up and breathed a sigh of relief. Then the eight band and crew members joined together onstage for our normal FFH prayer time.

During these moments we usually have a mini-devotional, then we pray for the concert. We pray that God will take us out of the way of what He is going to do—that people won't see the four of us on the stage, but they will see Jesus Christ. We pray that our pride will not get in the way, because we know that nothing we can do will change people's lives. Only God can do that kind of miracle. We pray that He will move in a huge way.

That night in Baker, Louisiana, our prayers seemed a little repetitious, but they were heartfelt. By the time we finished praying, we were behind schedule. We hurried to grab a bite to eat. Over dinner we talked and laughed and shared stories about the things we'd done the week before, almost forgetting the time. Then Matt—our road manager and the only guy who can keep all of us in line—sternly reminded us that we needed to get moving. We rushed to our dressing rooms and quickly changed into our concert clothes.

As we waited to go on, we began to feel the "we-haven't-done-a-concert-in-a-while" jitters. We had just gotten word that this was our biggest concert crowd ever, and we were pumped. The crowd seemed loud and rambunctious. We knew we had to give the performance of a lifetime.

Quickly we double-checked our cordless microphones and ear monitors. Then Matt came backstage and said, "Ready, guys?"

Suddenly Jeromy began to panic. "My mic is not working," he said, and he began yelling, "Check, check!" Matt grabbed the microphone and hurried off to the soundboard to get some help. At that point Michael began to panic too. He was having trouble with his ear monitors. He couldn't hear a thing.

The concert was already getting a late start, and now our technical difficulties were delaying it even more. We could hear the crowd becoming restless. Frantically, Allyson tried to fix the problems with new batteries, different frequencies, different antenna placements—anything she could pull out of her bag of tricks.

Matt returned with Jeromy's microphone.

"Check, check," Jeromy said. Nothing. A new battery had taken care of Mike's monitors, but the microphone was still dead. Matt and the crew scurried around like ants, trying everything they could think of to correct the problem. In all, it must have taken at least fifteen minutes to get up and rolling—but those fifteen minutes seemed like an eternity. *Could anything possibly go right from this point on? I thought. Was there even a crowd left?*

Finally we were introduced. "Please give a warm welcome to FFH!" we heard the announcer yell. *Here goes nothing,* I said to myself. But as we entered the stage, the crowd began screaming, and we could see a packed house through the spotlights. The crowd had been waiting for almost half an hour, and now their expectations were high. They were ready to be entertained!

Jeromy began singing, but his microphone went dead again. Thinking quickly, he grabbed Jennifer's mic, and we kept going. Then other things started to fall apart. Panic overtook us, and we all began to give frantic signs to Allyson, who was behind the monitor console. "Too much guitar." "No drums."

"More vocals." "I can't hear myself." The signs were flying fast and furious, and Allyson could barely keep up. We struggled to maintain some kind of stage presence even though our intensity had been sucked away by all the problems.

Still, the crowd seemed to stay with us, and about five songs into the show the technical difficulties finally got under control. But in our minds the damage had already been done. We had really messed up this concert!

The invitation time came, as it usually does, about halfway through the show. While Jeromy talked onstage, Jennifer and I quietly sneaked off. I had been waiting for this moment all night—a chance to get out of the spotlight and out of the nightmare, at least for a few minutes. Sweaty and worn out, Jennifer and I breathed a sigh of relief and made our way to the green room.

During the invitation time at FFH concerts, Jeromy shares his testimony with the crowd and explains what it means to have a personal relationship with Jesus Christ. Jennifer and I go backstage to avoid causing any kind of distraction. Then

Jeromy prays with the people in the audience who want to make decisions for Jesus.

That night Jeromy followed the normal pattern, and those who made decisions repeated a prayer of commitment with him. Then he told them how to start living out their new relationship with Christ. He encouraged them to follow Matt, who was standing down front, to a designated room so we could get their names and be able to pray for them later.

Jennifer and I knew this portion of the concert would be a little different tonight because Matt was going to have to escort the people through the backstage area. But what happened was not at all what we were expecting. As Jeromy told those who made decisions to follow Matt, they began to sing. With the first words of "God Is So Good," a commotion seemed to run through the audience, and dozens upon dozens of people began coming forward. Considering everything that had gone wrong that night, we could hardly believe our eyes!

Jennifer and I tried to make our way to the stage at that point, but there were no open paths in sight. Teenagers, young adults, kids, even grownups followed Matt backstage and lined the hallway to await their turns to fill out commitment cards and pick up some material to start them in their new-found faiths. Amazed and excited, we wound our way through the crowd of new believers, made it to our places onstage, and the second half of the concert got underway.

When the show was over, we learned that more than two hundred people had made decisions for Jesus Christ that night, which was close to a record for us. We were ecstatic! Even though numbers aren't what drive us to do what we do, it was wonderful to see so many lives changed.

Later that night I crawled into bed and began to relive the concert. I remembered how badly I had played and sung. I could vividly recall each note I had missed and each word I'd forgotten. I could remember everything that had gone wrong and every stupid thing I had done onstage. Technically and musically, the concert had been a flop. I felt bummed.

But then it dawned on me: Sure, we'd had a bad night, missed a few notes, sang poorly, and so on. It wasn't our best concert. It probably wouldn't even rank in the top two hundred! But something had happened that was better than anything we could have hoped for or imagined. Something had happened that night that changed people's lives. The Lord had moved in a big

People weren't saved because FFH did something. People were saved because God did something.

way, and more than two hundred people received eternal life. *Wow!*

I recalled the prayer we had prayed earlier in the day—that we would not get in the way of what only God could do, that the audience wouldn't even see us, and that God would move in a huge way. Well, God had answered. He did get us out of the way. The crowd certainly didn't come forward because we sang so well and put on such a great show! People weren't saved because FFH did something. People were saved because God did something.

I nodded off to sleep with a smile on my face. *That just may have been the best concert we've ever done, Lord,* I prayed. *Thank You for letting us be part of it.*

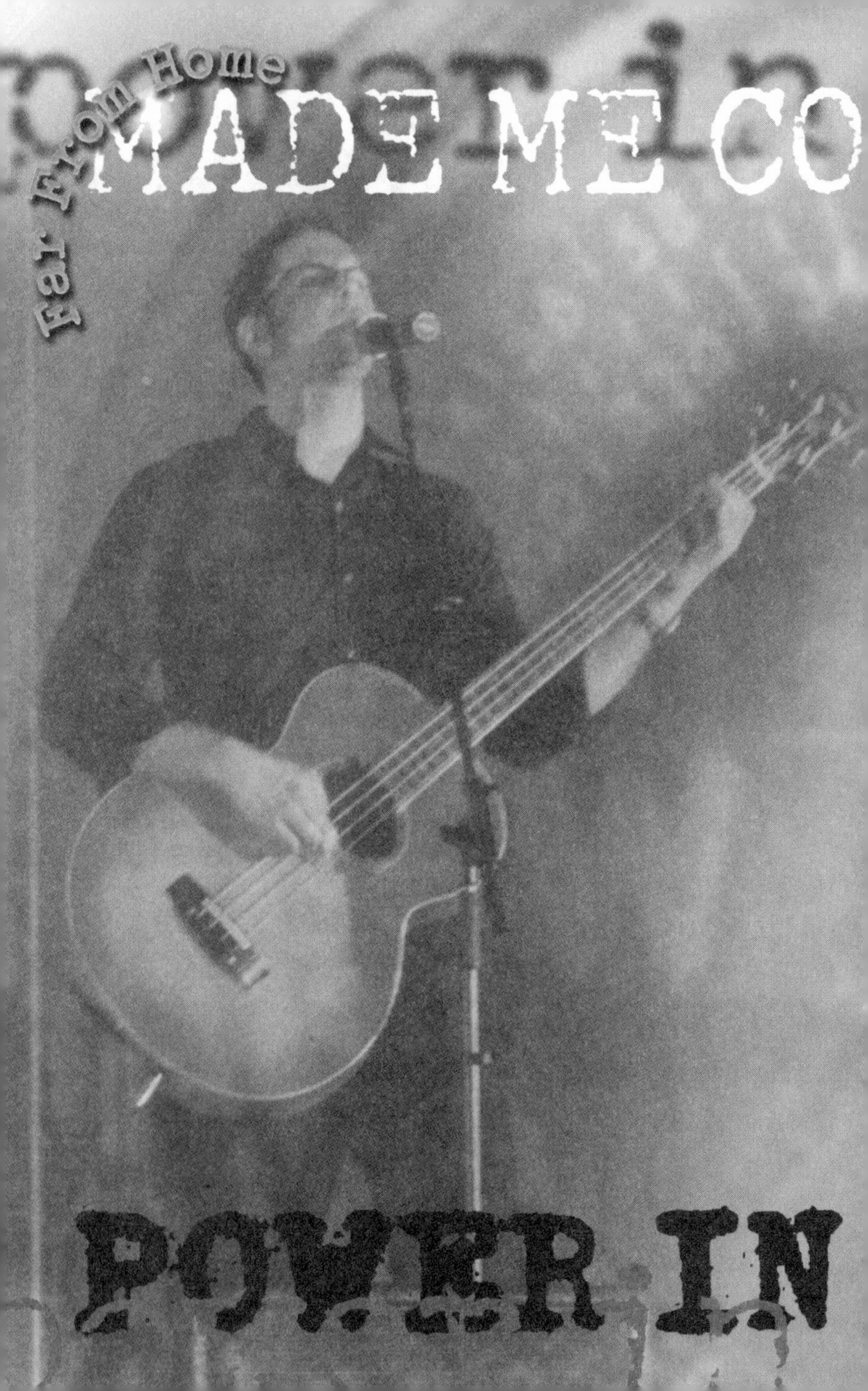
Far From Home
MADE ME CO
POWER IN

MPLETE

his blood

lead me home

You are the One
who has made me complete
Now I'm kneeling
at Your feet
Knowing only You can
lead me home
I'll stand through it all
Waiting on Your call
Knowing that **You'll hear**
my every prayer

You'll hear
my every
prayer

HIS BLOOD

Power in His Blood

Success God's Way

All of us in FFH learned an important lesson from that nightmare concert. When we're doing the things God has called us to do, the results are not up to us; they're up to God. And God's results are awesome! Even when we think we've messed it up, He is more than able to pick up our pieces and use them for His kingdom.

God measures success differently than we do. I thought our concert was a disaster because we'd made so many mistakes musically and technically. But God thought it was a monster show because He was able to move on so many hearts, unhindered by any pride or self-sufficiency on our part. The Bible says that all of heaven rejoices when just one person turns to Jesus. Seeing people get saved is much more exciting to God than listening to a flawless FFH concert!

All of us need to be willing to step into the background and let God move to the foreground, so He can work through us to do what only He can do. After all, as Christians our lives have been "hidden with Christ in God" (Colossians 3:3). When we humble ourselves and do what He tells us to do, God works through us in awesome ways. When we let pride get in the way and seek our own glory, however, we set ourselves up for disaster.

According to 1 Peter 5:5–6, "God opposes the proud but gives grace to the humble." The scripture continues: "Humble yourselves, therefore, under God's mighty hand, that he may lift you up in due time." I do not have to worry about the success of FFH. God will take care of that. My part is to humble myself before Him—and make sure I give Him all the glory.

What's Your Story?

1. How do you measure success? In what ways do you think your measure is different from God's?

2. Do you feel you must "toot your own horn" in order to get ahead in school, at work, or in life in general?

3. According to 1 Peter 5:5–6, what is God's response to our pride? What is His response when we show humility?

THIS is **love:**
NOT THAT WE loved God,
but **that** he loved us AND sent **his**
son as AN ATONING sacrifice
for **our** sins. DEAR FRIENDS,
since God so LOVED us,
WE also ought to **love** one another.
No ONE has EVER seen God;
but **if** WE LOVE ONE **another,**
GOD lives in us and
his love is made C O M P L E T E
in us.

—1 John 4:10–12

Angels in Disguise

Jeromy Deibler

One of the things I often take for granted about my job is the blessing of getting to meet so many wonderfully special people along the way: people who encourage me, people who make me think about my relationship with the Lord, people who cause me to be embarrassed that I sometimes complain about my life. Every night after a concert, as we board our bus and pull away from whatever venue we've played, the four band members and our crew pray together and share about the day. Almost always we talk about someone special we met…

Like Anna from Indiana. After the concert, she

proudly drove her wheelchair up to the autograph table using one hand and a joystick. She carried a press picture on her lap. She couldn't speak any words, but the sounds coming out of her mouth and the smile on her face told me of her joy. I grasped her hand and said, "Thank you for coming." She laughed. Her mom and dad stood behind her as we talked. You could tell that Anna was a special girl and that her parents loved her very much. They were glowing as she grinned from ear to ear.

We had our picture taken with Anna, and I signed her press picture. I told her how cool her chair was and how neat it was that she could drive it one-handed. I even asked if I could try the joystick. She laughed hysterically as I jerked the chair from side to side and then accidentally ran her into the table. As she pulled away and I turned my attention back to the autograph line, I wondered, *Why don't I have that kind of joy?*

Then there was Janna from Ohio. Janna was a beautiful woman, probably in her early thirties. She was stylishly dressed—in fact, she looked like she shopped with my wife, Jennifer. But she was alone and obviously upset. She waited around until almost everyone had left the building before approaching Jennifer and me. Janna explained that her husband had died less than six months before. He had been her whole life. They hadn't had any children. She didn't want to keep us, she said; she just wanted to tell us that our music, especially "One of These Days," had helped her through the grieving process. As she smiled and walked away, my heart sank into my stomach. Jennifer and I stared blankly at each other. *If something were to happen to Jennifer*, I thought, *I would probably grieve myself to death*. Janna's courage was inspiring.

We met Sissy in Baltimore. Every year our band played at her church—a come-as-you-are, anything-goes, jeans-and-T-shirt kind of church. Sissy was always the first one on her feet, clapping to the music. She was a vibrant woman who obviously loved the Lord. But Sissy contracted cancer. The disease eventually put her in the hospital and at the mercy of physicians. During our last visit to her church, some folks told us about her condition and asked if we would consider stopping by her hospital room to see her. We agreed, and after lunch we headed to the hospital.

We could tell immediately that Sissy was in pain. She smiled anyway as she saw us walk into the room and whispered to a friend who was kneeling by her bed, "Ask them to sing." As we started into an a cappella version of "View That Holy City," a smile came across her face. We sang a few more songs then left. She was still smiling as we walked out the door. *At that moment the Lord reminded me how precious life is and how often I take it for granted.*

Then there was Lanny, the bus driver. Lanny came to us in 1999. When our driver quit, someone suggested that we give Lanny a call. He had just finished traveling with a group he had been with for eighteen years, and he agreed to take our gig to help out short-term. It turned out we needed Lanny in more ways than one. During those few months he was with us, I had a nagging flu that made for some pretty interesting sets vocally. Frustrated and defeated after a show, I would drag into the bus, and Lanny would say, "Let's go." Together we would walk the forty-five feet to the back lounge of the bus, and he would pray. It always seemed to help.

I've never met anyone who loved Jesus more than Lanny. He never missed an opportunity to tell us how the Lord had worked in his life. After a long drive, other drivers would be on

the couch sleeping. Not Lanny. We'd find him shining the bus, praying over it and the people inside. Other drivers would be on their way to the hotel after dropping off the band. Lanny was setting up with the crew. *He taught me that God isn't into big-time stars; He just wants servants.*

We met Daryl at a concert at a church in Clarion, Pennsylvania. We had the opportunity to talk for a while over lunch and for a short time after the show. That next year we visited Clarion again, and Daryl was there, along with his family. After the show, Daryl and I sat on the back steps of the church and shared about our lives. He told me how the Lord was blessing his trucking company and how faithful God was toward him and his family. I shared some stories about God's faithfulness in my own life. Before we got up to leave, Daryl asked if FFH had any immediate needs. I told him about a few unpaid bills and about our desire to buy some new equipment in the upcoming months. He nodded as I told him that I wasn't worried about the money.

"God is faithful," I said. "He's taken care of our needs before, and He'll do it again."

We stood, and Daryl gave me a bear hug goodbye. That next week, a check for $7,500 arrived in the mail. It was from Daryl and his wife. They wanted to help with our expenses! *The Lord again reminded me that He is in control and that our money is His money.*

This list could go on and on. There are so many folks who have impacted my life, even after just a brief meeting. Like the woman in Mississippi who homeschools all ten of her children. Or the evangelist in Kentucky who was almost run out of town for starting a church. Or the promoter in Texas who nearly lost his job for allowing us to present the gospel to a group of teens. All of these people have

FFH wrote and recorded a jingle for Coca-Cola.

left their mark on me. I thank the Lord for allowing me to know them, and I pray that He will never let me forget the lessons I have learned through their touches on my life.

Whose Angel Are You?

Many believers today think they can worship God as "lone rangers." "I love God," they say, as they bounce from church to church (or never go to church at all); "it's Christians I don't like." But the Christian life was never meant to be lived alone. In fact, the New Testament is full of "one-another" commands: Love one another. Forgive one another. Encourage one another. Bear one another's burdens. Pray for one another. How can we obey the Word of God if we're not involved in the lives of other Christians?

According to the Bible, we are all—together— the body of Christ. We belong to one another. We need one another. Each of us has something to contribute, and no one is unimportant (see Romans 12:4–8; 1 Corinthians 12:12–31; and Ephesians 4:11–16). Are you in a wheelchair? You have an important place in the body of Christ. Are

I may never be a hero
Or set my feet on
Wall Street
Or give the evening news
But I believe in
what God wants me to be

you in a hospital bed? You have an important place in the body of Christ. Are you a bus driver, an entrepreneur, a mother, a student, a member of a band? You have an important place too. It doesn't matter how unimportant we feel. If we will just take our eyes off of ourselves and consider the needs of those around us, we can be impact players in the body of Christ.

Sometimes God does send angels from heaven as messengers and ministers. But you and I can be "angels" in each others' lives right now—blessing, supporting, and encouraging each other to become more like Christ. Hebrews 10:24–25 says, "And let us consider how we may spur one another on toward love and good deeds. Let us not give up meeting together, as some are in the habit of doing, but let us encourage one another—and all the more as you see the Day approaching."

Being an angel in someone's life doesn't have to take a lot of time. It may require only a simple touch. But by keeping the eyes of our hearts open and reaching out to other believers, we can impact one another's lives with the love of God.

What's Your Story?

1. Besides family and close friends, who are the "angels" in your life? Make a list of the people who have had an impact on you, even if their touch in your life has been fleeting or brief.

2. Have you ever been an "angel" in someone else's life? Do you look for opportunities to be a blessing in the lives of other Christians?

3. Do you feel unimportant in the body of Christ? Read Romans 12:4–8; 1 Corinthians 12:12–31; and Ephesians 4:11–16. Can the body of Christ "grow and build itself up in love" without your input?

Letters from the Road

Your song "Lord Move, or Move Me" has a very special meaning for my wife, who has cancer. The words of the song have given her hope to live. It seems to be made to encourage people with a life-threatening disease and to give them hope.

Thanks for the song, Lee

So if THE Son sets you free,
you **WILL** be
free indeed.

—John 8:36

Freedom behind Bars

Michael Boggs

9

As members of FFH, Jeromy, Jennifer, Brian, and I often have incredible opportunities to minister to people all across the world. Most of the time we stand in awe of God's wonderful work in our lives. But with as many dates as we play, sometimes life on the road can get a little repetitive and mundane; and if we're not careful, we can become numb to the opportunities God sets before us. Fortunately, whenever our focus is in danger of slipping, God usually throws something in our laps to remind us of who we are—and *whose* we are.

I got one of those "wake-up calls" during a

strenuous tour in the spring of 2000. Aaron Benward was on the road with us, and we were on our way to sing in a local prison. Aaron had ministered in prisons before. With great enthusiasm, he promised us that the day's experience would be a blessing not only for the inmates, but for us as well. I wanted to believe him, but to be honest, I was a little scared, a little excited, and very curious about what the day would actually be like.

We arrived on the prison grounds and entered the reception area. A few people were milling around nonchalantly—as if to show that what was behind those walls wasn't a big deal. But they didn't fool me. I knew some of the crimes the inmates had committed to get there!

A prison minister stepped up to greet us and told us a little bit about what was going to happen when we got inside "the yard." I listened intently, feeling at that point that I was holding up pretty well. A surge of bravery shot through my veins. But as soon as he concluded and said, "OK, it's time to go now," every drop of courage drained out, like air out of a balloon.

We were led to a room where a guard asked us to

empty our pockets. I was sure he could see the fear in my eyes as I dropped my wallet and a tube of Chap Stick into the designated bag. Then the thought came to me, *This is a lot like a security checkpoint in an airport, and I've been through plenty of those.* My muscles relaxed a little.

Unfortunately, my newfound comfort level didn't last long. A body search was next. As everyone who enters the prison yard must, we all got frisked for narcotics, guns, knives—anything that could be used as a weapon inside the prison. My fear increased exponentially. We all passed the check, of course, but I knew that the officers could see my timidity as I approached the doors leading to the outside.

Sticking close to the pastor, Aaron, and the other band members, I entered the yard, which looked like a big, open playground without any toys. Some of the inmates stared at us, and one young man called out something obscene to Brian, who was right next to me. My fear factor rose to an all-time high. The pastor gave us a brief smile and continued walking toward the prison building at the other end of the yard. I kept my eyes focused straight ahead. I was sure that if I didn't die immediately from this experience, I would die later from cardiac arrest once I realized where I'd been and what I'd done.

The tension eased a little as we approached the small gray building. An inmate who was working quietly in a nearby garden recognized the pastor, said hello with a grin, and returned to his work. His easy greeting was comforting somehow. Then we opened the door, and a totally different atmosphere seemed to rush out to greet us. To my surprise I could hear what sounded like praise-and-worship music coming from somewhere inside. As we walked down the hallway, the strains of "Amazing Grace" echoed through the corridor.

"What's going on? What are they doing?" I asked.

"The inmates are just finishing up a praise-and-worship service," the pastor explained. "You guys will go on fairly soon."

We turned the corner into a big room, and I couldn't believe my eyes. Hundreds of prisoners were singing worship songs, led by inmate musicians with guitars, drums, a piano, and a bass. We quickly found ourselves joining in. As the men closed their service with prayer, the pastor made his way to the podium and introduced Aaron and FFH. We grabbed our guitars and started playing a few of our songs just to loosen things up a bit—not so much for them as for us!

After a little while we moved into a praise-and-worship set. And I have to tell you, I have never been in a more awesome praise service! As the words "Oh, the blood of Jesus" rang out, it seemed as if God were standing right in front of us—as if we could reach out and touch Him. Next we sang "Power in His Blood," and some of the inmates begin to cry out loudly to God.

"Thank You, Jesus!" several shouted.

"Praise to the Holy One!" another exclaimed.

I had never experienced anything quite like this before. As I continued to play, I had to admit to myself that despite my initial trepidation, I was having the time of my life.

We wrapped up the service with a few more songs, Jeromy said a prayer, and we all put down our

Watching

Far From Home

all of the comfort You

Where could I go
where I don't know
All of the **comfort**
You bestow
Where could I fall,
Where could I land,
Where I'm not **resting**
In Your hand
How could I stray
TOO FAR AWAY

WATCHIN

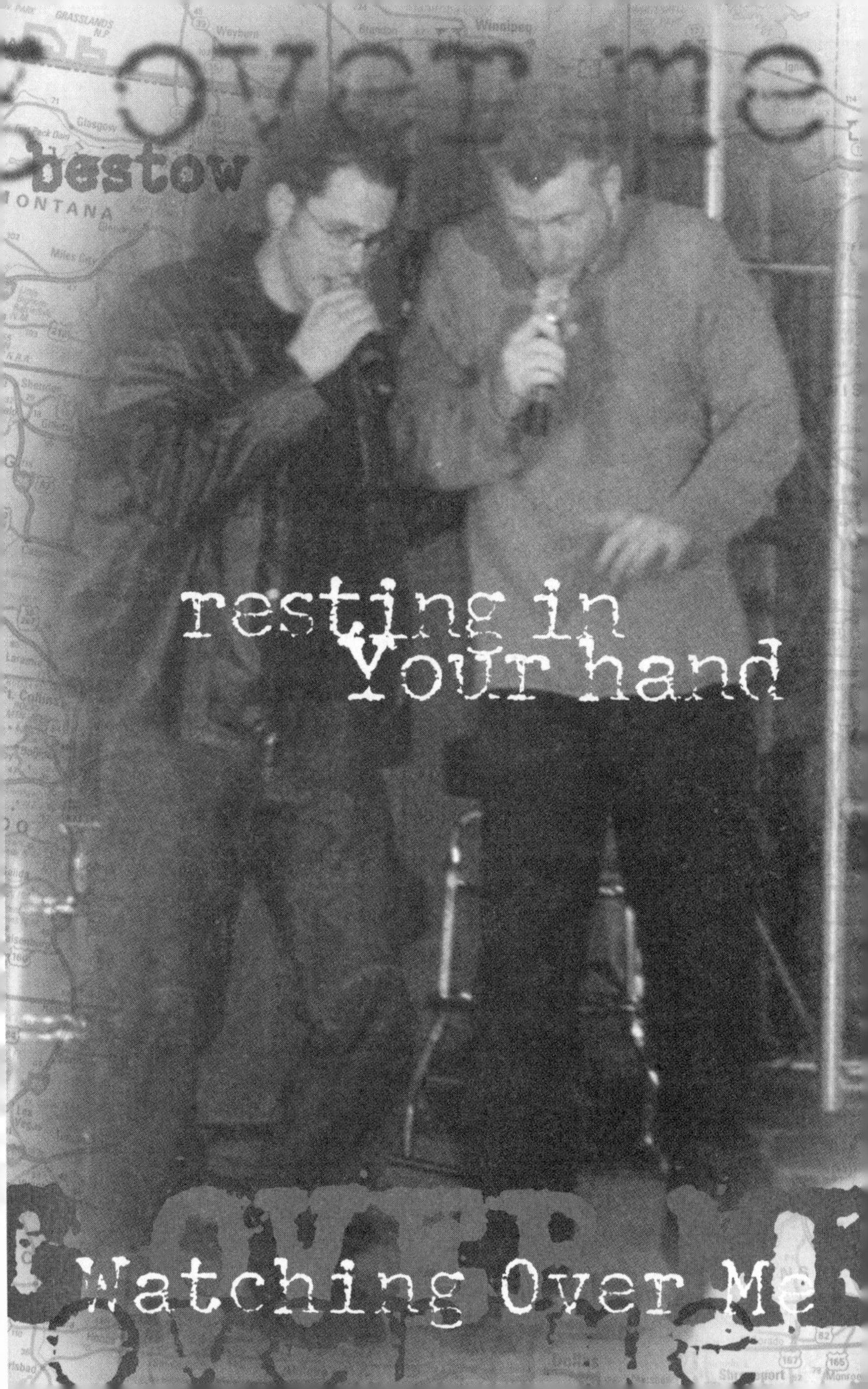
over me
bestow
resting in
your hand
Watching Over Me

guitars. But then Jeromy started to sing again. The song had only one word: "Amen." The whole room joined in. We must have sung that song for fifteen minutes or more. No one seemed to want to stop.

I was so amazed. These inmates who were praising God with such wonderful abandon were confined behind bars, closely watched, and guarded every moment of every day. Many of the men had been in prison for years. Yet through the grace of God, they had found freedom in Christ. Suddenly I began to feel a little guilty. Here I was, living on the "outside," able to come and go as I pleased. But did I have the freedom in Christ that they had? Was I as thankful for my salvation as they were? Was Jesus the most important thing in my life, as He was for these inmates? All they had was Jesus—but He was all they needed!

Silently I confessed my failures to God. I realized that I had become callous toward my salvation, and that callousness had become a hindrance to God's work in my life. *I desperately want to know You more intimately, like these men do,* I prayed.

As we said good-bye to the inmates, many of

them came up to us, hugged our necks, and told us that they loved us. Some men were crying; others were smiling from ear to ear; others thanked us profusely for making them a part of our day. "Keep on keeping on," some encour-

Many of the men had been in prison for years. Yet through the grace of God, they had found freedom in Christ.

aged. "Stay true to Christ," others said. Only hours before I had been wondering what I was doing in a prison, looking for ways to protect myself from the harsh realities that surrounded me. Now the very guys I had feared were complimenting us on a job well done and encouraging us in the Lord! I don't think I have ever felt as unworthy to be a minister as I did at that moment.

Now whenever I begin to get a little numb to what God is doing in and around me, I always remember that afternoon in the prison. God worked through me even though I wasn't completely ready to be used that day. And in the process I learned to appreciate the freedom I have to worship God and live every day for Him, thankful for the opportunities He gives me to minister through FFH. I also learned that freedom is not just a matter of being on one side of a prison wall or another. True freedom is found only in a living, breathing relationship with the One who sets us free.

The Truth Will Set You Free

Do you sometimes feel as if you've become numb to God's activity in your life? Do you feel as if you've missed opportunities to help others, to be a part of God's work, because you are bound by apathy, preoccupied with busyness, or held captive to a sense of unworthiness or fear? If so, you might want to pray a prayer like the one I said in the prison that day:

"Lord, forgive me for my inability to see You at work in my life. Forgive me for my callousness and my reluctance to do things for You and for others. Help me to keep my eyes on the path You have chosen for me, and give me the strength to follow it with complete abandon, no matter what the world does to try to block my way. I know You have set me free so I can live my life for You. As Proverbs 3:5–6 says, I will trust in You with all my heart, and I won't lean on my own understanding. I will acknowledge You in every way, knowing that You will direct my footsteps. Amen."

The truth is, you and I are constantly presented with opportunities to worship God and minister to the people around us. It doesn't matter what our circumstances are. We may feel stuck in school, at home, in an office, or in a factory. We may even find ourselves behind bars. But as Jesus said in John 8:32, "Then you will know the truth, and the truth will set you free." Jesus Himself is the Truth (see John 14:6). When we focus our lives on knowing Jesus and making our relationship with Him our top priority, He sets us free to be everything He has called us to be—and to minister to others in ways we could never imagine.

What's Your Story?

1. What does freedom mean to you? Do you feel free right now? Why or why not?

2. Describe a time when fear, apathy, or another emotion bound you and kept you from reaching out to someone who needed your help. What did you learn from that experience?

3. How can you know the truth that will "set you free"?

Letters from the Road

I know you probably get a lot of e-mails saying how much people have been touched by your music, but I thought that maybe God would use my story to touch your hearts.

I was married to a woman whom God placed in my life several years ago. When she was six months old she was diagnosed with cystic fibrosis. She attended public school, college, and a certification program in Cytotechnology —all against doctors' recommendations.

We met at Penn State University through Christian Student Fellowship and were married the next year. She was continually in and out of the hospital during our marriage. I spent many nights next to her in the hospital room while she received heavy-duty antibiotics.

Last year, we were told that the bacteria in her lungs was only sensitive to one antibiotic and that her immune system had become like an eighty-year-old's. The docs said we should consider a double lung transplant. So we started a fund-raising blitz to raise the money. The transplant was successful, but within a few days, she developed problems. They were finally able to stabilize her enough to move her back to intensive care, and I was able to talk to her.

She said she was scared, and I reassured her that God was in control and that there was nothing to worry about. I told her that I loved her and she said she loved me. Those were the last words I heard her say. For the next three weeks, the docs did all they could to help her. I sang to her and prayed that God's will would be done. I read Scripture to her and told her how much I loved her. At the memorial service I had "One of These Days" played—it was one of her favorites.

I miss her more than I thought I could. She was my best friend. Basically, I want to say thanks for encouraging me through your music. It has touched me very deeply, and I thank God for your willingness to serve Him. If you get the opportunity, would you think about me in your prayers? God is good even when His people are hurting. May He continue to bless you.

From my heart, Brad

Jesus replied: "**LOVE** the Lord **your God** with **ALL** your heart and **WITH** all your SOUL AND with all your M I N D." This is the **first** AND GREATEST commandment."

—Matthew 22:37—38

The Important Things

Jeromy Deibler

10

Do you know people who are always thinking about the future? Whose feet are walking in the present but whose minds are focused on things to come? Their eyes glaze over in long conversations because, in their minds, they have already left the room and moved on to the next thing. They make their homes in airports, and they live and die by their datebooks. Their state-of-the-art mobile phones hang loosely from their belts, and their cars are always just about out of gas. They sleep little, eat on the run, and think movies are a waste of time.

Any names come to mind? If not, let me give you

one: Jeromy Deibler. That's right—me. The stressed-out, future-driven control freak. I'm the poster child for Gary Smalley's "lion" personality. And I'm becoming less and less proud of it.

When FFH first came together in 1991, Brian and I were flying by the seat of our pants. We had a lot to learn and a lot of mistakes to make—and we were more than willing to make them. Onstage we were singing our teenage hearts out to anyone (and I mean *anyone*) who would listen. Offstage we were learning what strengths the Lord had given us and how we could use them in ministry together.

I quickly fit into the position of "visionary," and Brian took the "cleanup" role. Essentially, I envisioned the mess, made it, and then left Brian to clean it up! I made the phone calls, booked the dates (sometimes thirty-five shows in thirty days), handled PR and marketing, *and* created the music. Brian managed the money (if there was any), handled the taxes, organized the merchandise, and wrote the checks. We took turns driving the van, and we both helped with setup wherever we played.

It was a finely tuned system—for a while anyway.

As FFH progressed and the Lord allowed the intensity to be turned up on our ministry, things began to slip from my grasp. Shows for fifty people turned into shows for five hundred and then fifteen hundred. Youth group newsletter interviews turned into national magazine articles. We went from a van to a motor home to a bigger motor home to a bus. We were invited to radio shows and TV appearances, record-label parties and music conventions. And the responsibility for scheduling and arranging everything was all mine. The pressure I felt was huge.

It wasn't long before my marriage was suffering, my performance was weakening, and my spiritual life was on a downward spiral. I had become like my car—continually running on almost empty.

I can vividly remember the day all the pressure came to a final boil. We had just performed an acoustic set at a Dove Awards press conference in Nashville. With the event winding down, I retreated to a corner with my cell phone to talk to a friend and business partner about how to finance FFH's spring tour. I was pretty frustrated by the time I got off the phone.

On the way home that afternoon, in the middle of an argument with Jennifer (in which I was undoubtedly in the wrong), I got the voice mail that broke the proverbial camel's back. Our booking agent said he needed me to fax him commitments right away on a number of booking offers that I hadn't even looked at yet. It was a small request, really, but I knew it meant another night in my office—a night that should be spent with my wife. By the time Jennifer and I sat down to dinner I was utterly defeated, almost in tears.

"The stress is getting to be unbearable," I told her. "If something doesn't break, I'm going to."

Jennifer, of course, had seen this coming. When I finished telling her everything that was weighing on me, she sensitively—but very sternly—told me what needed to be done.

The very next day FFH made some big changes. We hired a manager, and the manager hired a publicist. I made a commitment to read my e-mail less and my Bible more. I decided that my relationships with Jennifer, my family, and, most importantly, the Lord would take constant precedence over my involvement in FFH.

Do you remember the story about Martha and Mary in Luke 10:38–42? Martha was the sister who was always rushing around, constantly distracted by all the little details of life. Mary, on the other hand, had her priorities straight. She knew what the important things were. And she knew that the most important thing of all was taking time to sit at the feet of Jesus. Well, I was tired of being Martha, I decided. I was ready to be Mary for a change!

At that point in time, the Lord seemed to turn the page into a new chapter in my life—one that is still being written. It's a new and exciting chapter, but it's also one of deep and abiding peace. I'm finally understanding, maybe for the first time, what the important things are.

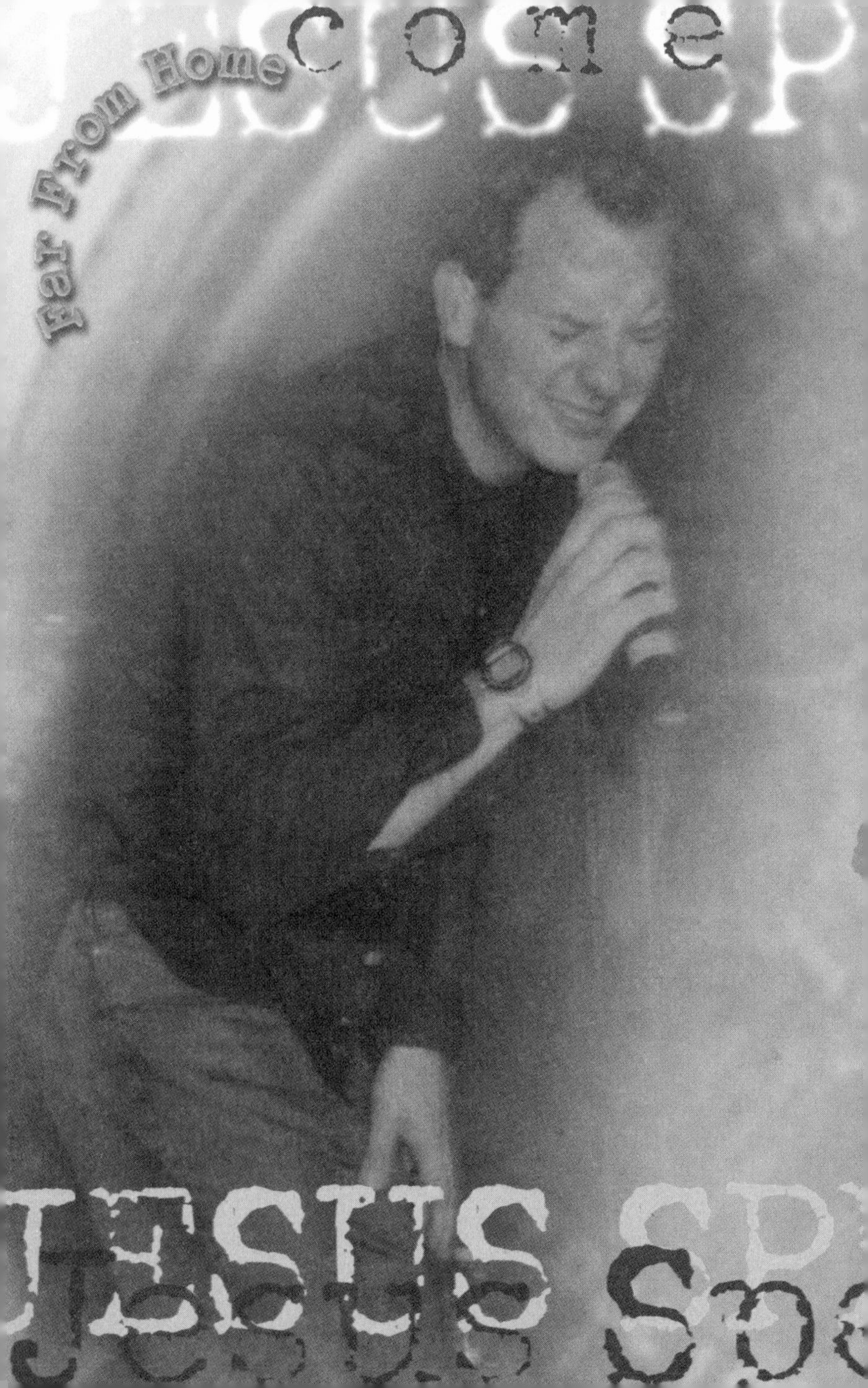

Far From Home
JESUS

Feels like I'm losing my mind
GOING CRAZY
Feels like I'm
running out of time
Come and save me
Just wipe the tears
from my eyes
Say it's alright,
ALRIGHT

come and
save
say it's alright
alright

Jesus Speak to Me

God's Greatest Desire

God loves it when we labor with Him in the work of His kingdom. According to 2 Corinthians 5:18, He has called us to take an active part in His "ministry of reconciliation" to a lost world. He rejoices when we bear "fruit that will last" (John 15:16). But what God desires more than our work *for* Him is that we have an intimate relationship *with* Him.

Our God—the one who numbered the stars and formed us from the dust—is also the God whom Jesus told us to call "Father." And you can be sure that our heavenly Father did not create us to be stressed-out ministry slaves. He created us to fellowship with Him as His precious children and then, out of gratitude for His unending love and saving grace, to partner with Him in His work.

It has taken me twenty-five years to begin to understand what put Mary at the Savior's feet and kept Martha in the kitchen. But the Lord is patiently teaching me what is important in life and what is not. Just as Mary knew that time *with* Jesus was more important than time *for* Jesus, the Lord wants us to understand that He desires our attention more than our energy—our time more than our timecard. And the amazing thing is that out of that intimate time spent with the Father, we find the right motivation and the ultimate power for effective ministry.

What's Your Story?

1. Whom do you identify with most, Mary or Martha?

2. Have you ever been so caught up in activities and busywork that you neglected your relationship with the Lord? How did you that make you feel?

3. Make a list of those things in your life that always seem to take precedence over time spent with God. What changes can you make to get your priorities straight?

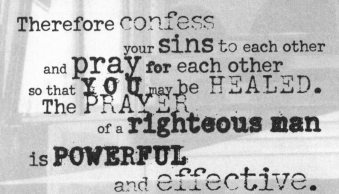

Therefore confess your **sins** to each other and **pray** for each other so that **you** may be HEALED. The PRAYER of a **righteous man** is **POWERFUL** and effective.

—**James 5:16**

Thomas

Jennifer Deibler

11

We meet so many people on the road that, unfortunately, names and faces start to run together after a while. (I wish that didn't happen, but I guess our memory banks can only hold so much!) Sometimes, though, a name and a face will jump out of the crowd and stick with us for a long time. That's what happened for me one rainy day in South Carolina during our Found a Place tour.

We woke up late that morning. Despite the overcast skies, the Carolinas were as beautiful as ever. We didn't get to enjoy the view for long, however, because we had to hurry off the bus to get to an autograph-signing event at the local Christian bookstore. Afterward we headed to the church where the concert was being held that night, did our sound check, and ate dinner quickly so we could get ready for the show. The concert went well, from what I can remember. I have to admit the details are fuzzy. But what happened after the concert is something I don't think I will ever forget.

We were on our way to the autograph table after the show when our road manager, Matt, told us that a young boy who had cancer wanted to meet us. Did we want to say hello to him and his family privately before we headed out to greet the rest of the crowd? Of course, we agreed. It is not uncommon for us to meet people who are sick or disabled—those who would have difficulty navigating through a crowd or waiting in a long line—before meeting with everybody else.

Matt ushered us into a big room that was empty except for little Thomas and the family members surrounding him. I had to do a double take. Little Thomas looked strikingly similar to my nephew, Zachary. He was about the same age as Zachary and just as adorable. My heart broke as I realized what a struggle this cute little guy was having to go through at such a young age. Cancer is hard enough for adults to deal with; how difficult must it be for this nine-year-old boy?

Then a terrifying thought came to me: *What if Zachary were the one with cancer? What if he were as sick as Thomas is right now and there was nothing I could do to help him get better?* The idea was almost more than I could bear. I wanted to go right over, scoop up Thomas into my arms, and tell him that everything was going to be all right. It *had* to be all right!

I held back, however, and let Jeromy and the other band members lead the way across the room. Even though my heart went out to Thomas, I was afraid. These kinds of situations are always so hard for me. What if I make the wrong move, say the wrong thing, and make everybody feel uncomfortable? I was glad at that moment that Jeromy was with me. He is never at a loss for words, and he tends to take over at such times.

Jeromy broke the ice first, and then we all began introducing ourselves. Afterward we gathered in a circle to pray for Thomas. We all bowed our heads, but I didn't close my eyes. I just watched this brave little boy as he accepted our prayers with a smile. *What his tiny body must be suffering!* I thought to myself. *What this family who loves him must be suffering!* I could barely hold back tears.

Jeromy finished praying, and we signed CDs and T-shirts for Thomas and the others before Matt rushed us off to the autograph table. For the next hour I smiled and signed my name for the people in line, but I couldn't get my mind off of Thomas.

"I can't stop thinking about that poor little boy," I whispered to Jeromy. He nodded, and we both kept signing.

Later that night, after all the equipment and merchandise was loaded onto the bus, the group gathered for prayer as we usually do before going to bed. We prayed for all of the people who got saved that night, for safety on the drive to the next city, and for several other requests. My prayer was for Thomas. In fact, for many nights afterward, my prayer continued to be for Thomas. It seemed that the Lord kept bringing him and his family to my mind.

My dad always told me that if someone comes to your mind out of the blue, then you need to pray for that person. It could be that God is placing them on your heart for a reason. It has been more than a year since the day I met Thomas

We all bowed our heads, but I didn't close my eyes. I just watched this brave little boy as he accepted our prayers with a smile.

in South Carolina, and God continues to remind me of him. Every time I think of him, I say at least a short prayer. In fact, Jeromy and I have a picture of Thomas on our refrigerator as a reminder to pray. We also have a letter from Thomas's mother asking anyone who might read it to pray—not just for her son's healing, but for God to be glorified through their situation.

A couple of weeks ago, Jeromy and I became curious about how Thomas was doing. His mother had included a phone number at the bottom of her letter, so we decided to call. I have to admit I was a little afraid of what we might hear.

I nervously fixed lunch while Jeromy talked to

Thomas's mom. I listened to the one-sided conversation, trying to figure out what was going on based on the things Jeromy was saying or not saying. Finally he hung up and sat down at the table with me to eat lunch. Between bites he told me that Thomas was doing quite well. He was feeling good, and his cancer was in remission. The doctors were not willing to declare him cancer-free; they couldn't do that until he had been in remission for seven years. But for now, there were no signs of the disease!

Thomas is ten now. Hopefully the cancer will stay in remission and by the time he graduates from high school, he won't have to worry about being sick anymore. In the meantime, I'm going to keep praying for Thomas. And if you feel led to pray for him, I know your prayers would be greatly appreciated.

Prayer That Moves Mountains

To me, prayer is one of the greatest privileges of being a Christian. Because Jesus' sacrifice on the cross cleared the way for us to be in a right rela-

Jennifer's favorite Bible passage is Ephesians 2:8–9.

tionship with God, we can pray with confidence, knowing that our heavenly Father loves us and hears us and wants to answer our prayers.

What is prayer? Simply put, prayer is communication with God. It is talking to Him freely about the things that are on our hearts. It doesn't require lots of big, flowery words or King James English. In fact, sometimes it doesn't require words at all! In prayer, we simply talk naturally to God as we would to a best friend—a very special Best Friend, of course, who has the power to move mountains and change circumstances that we cannot budge.

First John 5:14–15 says, "This is the confidence we have in approaching God: that if we ask anything according to his will, he hears us. And if we know that he hears us—whatever we ask—we know that we have what we asked of him." During the last year I have gone often to my heavenly Father to ask Him to heal Thomas and to glorify Himself through that situation. I know that He has heard every prayer. And I have faith that He is working out His best for Thomas right now.

When I thirst,
You will **quench me**
When I hunger,
You are the
bread for me
When I kneel,
You already **heard me**
You are there for me
**You're always
there for me**

when you thirst
quench
me
when I
kneel
you
already
heard me
want to h

What's Your Story?

1. What is your definition of prayer? How has your definition affected the way you pray or how often you pray?

2. When you pray, do you have confidence that God hears you? Why or why not?

3. Make a list of the "mountains" that are in your life right now. Ask God to work out His best for you and your loved ones in those situations.

Letters from the Road

Dear FFH,

Last year a friend and coworker gave me your CD I Want to Be like You. At the time, I set it aside. Two days after receiving the CD, my husband, Paul, passed away unexpectedly. As I was sitting home alone just a few days after Paul's death, I remembered receiving your CD from my friend. I placed it in the CD player.

As I listened to "One of These Days," tears flowed down my cheeks and my heart was deeply touched. The words reassured me that my husband was now able to "see the hand that took the nails for him," "hold the key to the mansion that was built for him," "walk the streets of gold that were paved for him," and "see his Savior face to face." What a beautiful song.

Two years have passed since Paul took the hand of Jesus; your song continues to bring me peace, comfort, and inner joy. In my mourning, your song brought me healing. May God continue to bless your ministry and touch the hearts of many. Thank you! I look forward to seeing you as your touring brings you to my town.

With Christ's love,
Anna

Now we KNOW that if the **EARTHLY TENT** we LIVE in is destroyed, we have a **building from God,** an E T E R N A L house in heaven, NOT built by human hands.

—2 Corinthians 5:1

The Homecoming

Brian Smith

12

We had just finished a concert in Toledo, Ohio. It had been a good show—everything had gone smoothly, and the crowd had been receptive. So far, everything about the Spring 2000 tour was going great. Lots of people were showing up, and many were surrendering their lives to Jesus. That night's concert had been no exception.

After the concert we went through our typical routine of loading all the gear on the sound truck and then counting and loading the merchandise. My wife, Allyson, and I took showers (it's so nice when a venue is equipped with them!), and the rest of the band began cleaning up too. Tired but refreshed, Allyson and I boarded the bus, looking forward to a perfect night of sleep during the long drive to our next concert.

We waited in the front lounge of the bus for the rest of the group so we could have our regular time of prayer. When FFH is on the road, we always meet before going to bed so we can pray as a group for those who made commitments that night, for the drive ahead, and for any other prayer requests we might have. Jeromy and Jennifer had been the last ones to hit the showers, so we weren't surprised to find ourselves waiting for them. That was OK; we were in no hurry. The rest of us just hung around, talking and munching on snack food.

It was about midnight when I glanced out the window and saw Jeromy and Jennifer finally making their way to the bus. Jeromy was carrying all his wife's bags, as usual, and they loaded them in the underneath compartment. As Jeromy stepped into the bus, however, I noticed a weird look in his eyes—bewilderment, disbelief, *something*.

"I have some bad news," he said, sitting down in

front of me. The entire bus was suddenly quiet. A good friend of ours had been killed in a car crash earlier that evening, he said. He had just gotten the call. She had died on impact.

At that moment, the lounge of the bus seemed to stand still. It was surreal—any movement appeared to be in super-slow motion. Jeromy and I just stared at each other, and Allyson's eyes filled with tears. We couldn't believe it. We had known Linda practically all our lives. Her son Chad was a childhood friend of ours. In fact, he was one of the original members of FFH. He helped start this thing!

That night I couldn't sleep. I kept thinking about Linda, the crash, their tight-knit family, and everyone back home in Pennsylvania. Memories swept across my mind like film through a projector. I remembered the many dinners I ate at Linda's house with Chad and his twin brothers. I remembered practicing in Linda's living room and giving her sneak previews of our new music. I remembered listening to her sing at church and at camp meetings. She had a beautiful voice, and her crisp, clean soprano would cut through on songs like "Home Free" and "Precious Memories."

She was an inspiration to everyone who knew her—
an amazing testimony to Jesus Christ, and everything
a godly mom should be.

And in an instant, she was gone!

Every day that week I tried to gather enough
courage to call Chad and let him know that we were
praying for him and his family. Finally I picked up
the phone and dialed. When I heard Chad's voice
on the other end, my heart sank in my chest. What
pain my friend must be experiencing! After saying
hello and making a bit of small talk, the conversation quickly became emotional. Chad told me
about the accident, repeating what I'd already heard
but in greater detail. He said that his mom had been
driving down Route 222 toward Willow Street to
meet her husband and sons for dinner when the
crash occurred. I could picture the exact location in
my head. Shortly after the collision, her husband
and sons drove along the same route, expecting to
meet Linda at the restaurant. That's when they saw
the wreckage and recognized her car in the middle
of it. It was a horrifying moment.

Chad shared with me how his father and brothers were doing now and how he was doing. I could hear the heartache in his voice as he struggled to finish his sentences. Then, before we ended our conversation, he said something that floored me.

It's strange how something that happened so far away could hit so close to home.

"If someone would have told me two weeks ago that my mom was going to die, it would have torn me apart," he said. "But God has given me and my family a peace and comfort that we can't even understand. We just want this to be a testimony to Mom's life and to her faith in Jesus Christ."

As I hung up the phone, Chad's final words stuck with me. After all his family had been through—after losing their beloved wife and mother in a tragic crash—they just wanted their reaction to be a testimony to her life and to her relationship with Jesus! That blew me away. I knew Chad and his family were heartbroken; yet God was working miraculously in their lives. Only He could provide such comfort— and the kind of peace that "transcends all understanding" (Philippians 4:7).

I have never been the same since that accident. It's strange how something that happened so far away could hit so close to home. Chad's family was similar to my family; his relationship with his mom was similar to my relationship with my mom. I guess you could say we were both momma's boys! Many nights I've lain awake, wondering what I would do if I lost my mother. How would I function? Would I have enough faith to rest in God's peace, like Chad did?

As I think about the accident now, I am comforted by one thing: I know that Linda loved Jesus. Because of her faith in Christ, I know she arrived that April morning at her ultimate home in heaven. And what a homecoming it must have been! Now she is spending eternity with her Savior. How wonderful it is to rest in the love of Jesus Christ, knowing that He has prepared a place for everyone who puts their faith in Him.

Brian's favorite verse is Colossians 3:17.

Heavenly Reservations

One of the best things about being a Christian is knowing without a doubt that you will spend eternity with Jesus. In fact, if you are a believer, there is a place reserved in heaven just for you. How do I know? Jesus said so! When the day of His arrest and crucifixion drew near, Jesus told His disciples that He would be leaving them soon. This was very upsetting news to His twelve friends. What would they do without Jesus? How could they go on with their lives without Him?

But Jesus comforted them with these words: "Do not let your hearts be troubled. Trust in God; trust also in me. In my Father's house are many rooms; if it were not so, I would have told you. I am going there to prepare a place for you. And if I go and prepare a place for you, I will come back and take you to be with me that you also may be where I am" (John 14:1–3).

The good news is our Father's house has many rooms. The bad news is we all know people who

Breath for my body,
light for my eyes
All that I need
You daily provide
Deep in my being,
more than my blood
My very existence
depends on
Your love

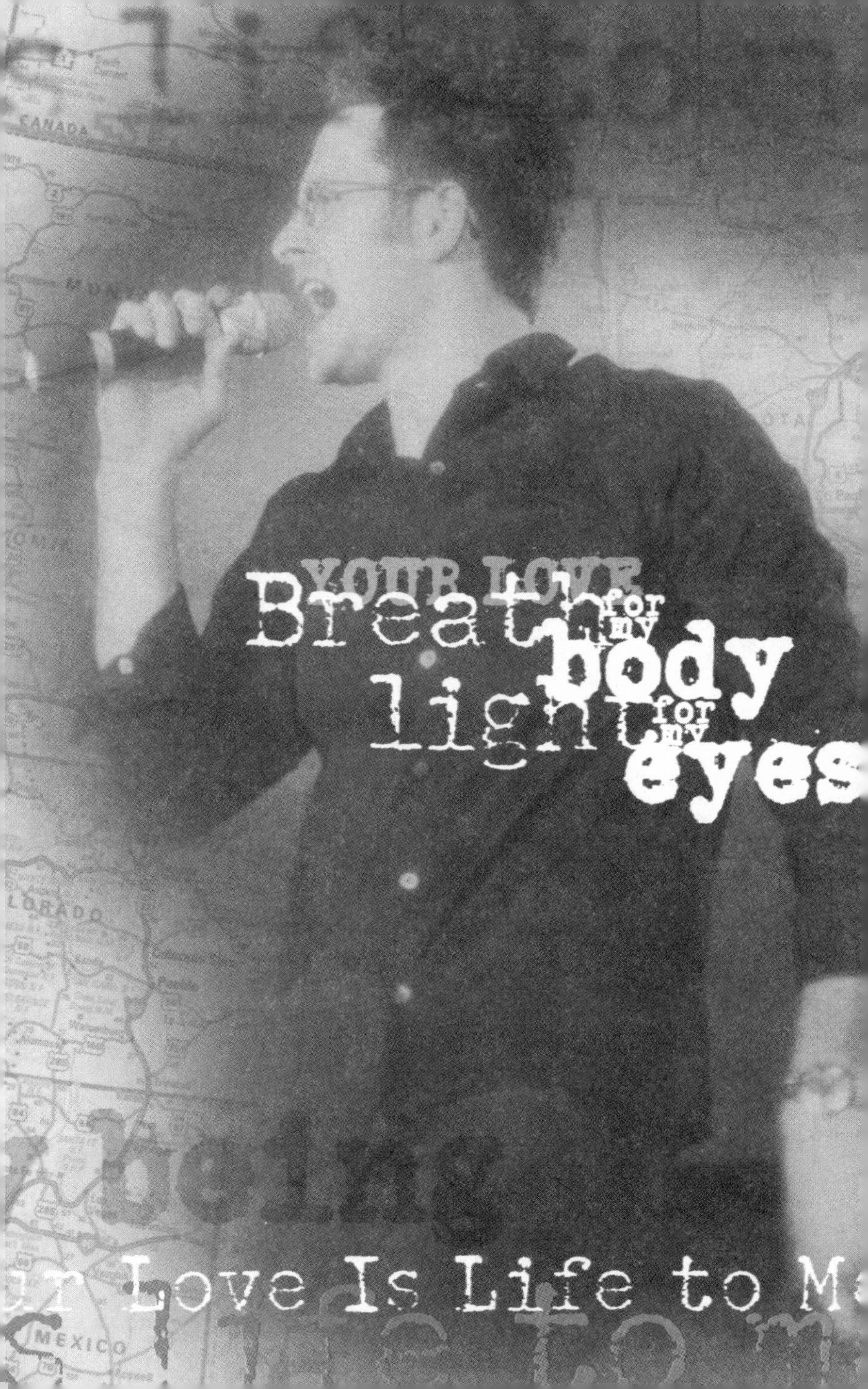
CANADA
YOUR LOVE
Breath for my body
light for my eyes
ur Love Is Life to M
MEXICO

haven't made their reservations yet. I don't know about you, but just thinking about heaven makes me want to tell others about it. I want all my friends and loved ones to be there with me! Is there someone you need to tell about heaven—and about the One who wants to prepare a place there just for them?

What's Your Story?

1. Do you know without a doubt that you will be spending eternity with Jesus?

2. What do you think heaven will be like?

3. Think of the names of two or three loved ones who need to know how to have eternal life in Christ. Commit to praying for them, and ask God to open up an opportunity for you to talk to them about Jesus.

Letters from the Road

Dear FFH,

Your song "One of These Days" reminds me that I will one day be with Him. It also reminds me of my brother. He died when he was just two years old of a cancer called neuroblastoma. It is a children's cancer. Your song reminds me that I will one day see him again. Thank you for spreading God's love.

In His name,

JoAnn

Signature vocals and acoustic-driven pop melodies have made FFH one of the most recognized young groups in Christian music. With more than 500,000 in career record sales, multiple radio #1's, magazine cover stories, and headline tours nationwide, FFH has achieved what most would consider success. But for the four members, who cling passionately to their mission statement to reach as many people for Jesus Christ as they can, as quickly as they can, their greatest reward is watching families attend their shows together and seeing people come to know Christ.

FFH's latest release, *Have I Ever Told You,* includes "Watching Over Me" and the inspirational "On My Cross" and is available wherever great music is sold.

www.ffh.net